Looking Life in the Eye

Poets of Central Florida
Volume Three

"Poetry is when an emotion
has found its thought and
the thought has found words."
~ Robert Frost

Looking Life in the Eye

Poets of Central Florida
Volume Three

A Contemporary Anthology

Elaine Person, Russ Golata,
Gary Broughman, editors

CHB Media
Publisher

ISBN 978-0-9863842-3-3
LIBRARY OF CONGRESS CONTROL NUMBER: 2015937649

CHB MEDIA, PUBLISHER

(386) 690-9295
chbmedia@gmail.com
www.chbmediaonline.com

First Edition
Printed in the USA

TABLE OF CONTENTS

Introduction

The Poets

Introduction

I have never been more proud of a book published by CHB Media than I am of this third volume in the Poets of Central Florida series, *Looking Life in the Eye*. One hundred of the best poets in Central Florida are represented, along with the diversity which is poetry today. The practice of poetry is prospering on many levels, from live venues in coffee houses and bars, to classes and writing groups in libraries, and of course through the state organization, Florida State Poets Association, which draws its strength from Central Florida and will host the 2015 National Conference in St. Petersburg.

We know that the Poets of Central Florida anthologies have added to the growth of poetry in Florida. For one, by combining poets from the East Coast with those of Greater Orlando, we helped introduce the two communities to each other and helped initiate a powerful alliance. This year's third volume in the series also includes several fine poets from the Gulf Coast of Central Florida. So the expansion in the anthology is not only in the number of poets but also geography.

The Poets of Central Florida series was actually born in a conversation in early 2010 between myself and my friend "Twinkle" Marie Manning. We had turned a launch party for my new novel into a celebration of original poetry and music from local artists. The excitement of the event inspired Twinkle to suggest CHB Media publish a contemporary anthology of Central Florida poets. I followed her idea to a number of open mics, like Badass Coffee in Orlando and Java Jungle in Port Orange. There I met the poets, including longtime host Russ Golata, and Elaine Person—my co-editors on this project.

I love the poetry in this book. All kinds of styles from all kinds of poets, all serious about their poetry—and *Looking Life in the Eye* through this wonderful art.

Gary Broughman
CHB Media

Louise Witzenburg
Lake Mary

BACKYARD ART

While I slept, a spider spun its universe.
Harnessed fast between the trunks of two live oaks,
precisely-woven strands of silk
form bridges, ladders. hub and spokes,
foundation lines and traps.
Its spinning done, the spider rests
and waits the flare of sun
to sprinkle web with diamond chips
and bits of amethyst.
Like moth drawn to the heart of flame,
an insect is bewitched
by ribbons, spirals, arcs and beads.
I watched the spider race across
the web to outer rim
and greet its guest with vicious kiss
that took its breath away.
No prayers to court of last resort
can save the hapless prey
from ravishment and ordained death
on parlor's hackled strands.

Louise Witzenburg

EPIPHANY

I watch the bright red tulips bloom
and shiver as I realize that I am witness
to the force that turns the Wheel of Life.
I am no less than tulips.
I, too, shall thrive, endure and rise
and meet with regained passion
the promise of tomorrow.

Al Rocheleau
Orlando

BOMBING THE MUSES

I am sick of answering to clichés.
Of awaiting the uninevitable.
These are after all, not
the women you marry.
One carries asps in her purse.
Another folds the arsenic
into raisin bread, and butters.
Her sister lays perfect spikes
under a slip of gardenias;
another wrinkles the mind.
When the hollow one laughs at you
you're too embarrassed
not to laugh back.
The dancer will not trace your instep
or help you when you fall.
These are the coveted apparencies
that perform tricks
when well fed,
that pretend to scream of satisfaction
but after, they fish the wallet
for cards and open accounts.
The muse you keep is the one you love,
more than yourself, and not finding her
you break into the sorority
after midnight,
and crush them
all with lamps.

Al Rocheleau

A MARRIAGE

Sometimes what is said ends a season.

We are a threshed field
rolling to the boundary line.

The stubble writhes in winter wind
then sleeps beneath a warm
mantle of snow.

We're the picturesques
framed in the small parlor
of a farmer in the dell.

We put ourselves
through the misery of planting,
the want, the waiting, a hell.

And then, just as accounts
come due, the hour strikes
its ever-eleven
and the almanac portends

we grow into the subtle rain
and all is well.

Peter Gordon
Orlando

TO MY SON BECOMING A FATHER NEXT MONTH

Twenty-eight years ago
I was twenty-eight
You were twisting and dancing
in your mother's womb
to tunes played on phonograph records

Today I see you sit on your bed
watching your wife's womb whirl
while your son dances within her
as you play guitar and sing

worlds of possibilities
reach through open windows
to wrap you and your family
in a shining future

I wish you bright tunes
high harmonies and
that one day you, too
may stand where I stand now

Peter Gordon

DOO WOP WEDDING

Come go with me to the aisle
Little star, paint a portrait of my love
With this ring, this I swear
You belong to me

Tonight, tonight
Stay in my corner
Come softly to me
In the still of the night

Why do fools fall in love
I've cried before
Tears on my pillow
My true story

Lucinda, I'll never tell
You know you're doing me wrong
Don't knock, baby tell me
What am I living for?

The magic touch
Little darling
Oh what a night
Will you still love me tomorrow?

Cherelyn Bush
Palm Coast

TRUE BEAUTY

We know as women
the significance of a wedding
A man and woman
joining together into one
The series of steps
that led to that moment
The progression of feeling
that led to a proposal
An engagement and
waiting for the day
Sisters all when sharing
the knowledge
Don't outshine the bride
But there she was
in her vintage dress
and bald fluffy head
Just shining with her
hard won survival
The most beautiful woman
at the wedding

Cherelyn Bush

FEARLESS LEADER

How could you be felled by your heart
So kind and open
Who was there to help you
At the attack
Why were there no warnings
To alert your doctor
What did you think
As we all wondered "where ..."
When did you know you would remain
Our fearless leader

Peter Meinke
St. Petersburg

MY FATHER

has just had a hip replacement
successful but
with a long siege of therapy

to come because he already
has one plastic kneecap
and a wooden leg from a mine

he stepped on at Anzio
It seems also he's
a candidate for a new heart

and when that occurs
I'll visit him although
we never got along but hey

I'll bring him a nose
and a moustache too and by God
we'll just say

the magic word

Peter Meinke

POEM ON YOUR BIRTHDAY
—for Jeanne

We always love the poem we're working on
we like the sounds of it
consonants and vowels
floating off our ballpoint pens
as if they were going somewhere important

Right now I'm so excited
by this very poem
I have to summon your soft touch
to calm me down
After all   we remind ourselves
tomorrow we may not like it so much

But it's no use: I love it today
with my primitive heart
wingless as an apteryx
Hey poem bound down to me
Make this day a special day:
the twenty-fifth of March
two thousand and six

Alice Friedman
Fern Park

LEAVING FOR A MEETING

I'd better take it just in case I need it
then if I need it I will be so glad I brought it
but I shouldn't need it and
if I don't take it I won't waste time
wading through what I don't need
never to find what I am looking for.

And
if I know I didn't take it
I'll know I don't have it
then I won't look for it
and that will lighten my load.

Alice Friedman

THE WALL

Blue cornflowers scattered in a yellow field
exhale stripper-soaked fumes.
A corner curl of attitude gives way
to reveal coils of anger.
Peel off ribbons of pride.
Another edge is stuck
more stripper
more scraping
beneath the anger
Fear.
The air is stripper saturated dizzy
wet-fear-mush disintegrates
to little scraps and crumbles.
The last chunks of fear-clutched-blue cornflowers
fall to the floor.
What now   courage?

Leslie C. Halpern
Oviedo

FRIENDLY FIRE

Primary mission if I choose to accept it:

Mingle among the maze
until I zero in on my target.
Squint eyes scanning room for clues.
Use heat-seeking missiles
with high-tech night vision
and sophisticated secret weaponry,
to help find him in the crowd.

Feel his gaze upon me
and lock onto his position
from across the room.
Then exchange breathless seconds
of friendly fire
during our love and war games,
before retreating to our secondary missions.

Leslie C. Halpern

SECRET RITE

With lightning speed
she jumps over
magic leaves that
glow red throughout
the autumn night.
Her secret rite
fuels the flame of
superstitious fire.

Hidden among
shadows and light,
she calls upon
ancient powers,
Egyptian myths,
to overcome
realities
and maladies.

There's no need to
medicate or
meditate, for
her leaps of faith
subordinate
body and mind.
With spirit cured,
salvation's assured.

First published in Connections: A Collection of Poems, 2008.

Wanice Blume
Orlando

A PLACE IN FLORIDA

I grew up in Indiana
Where it's cold 'til winter's done
My husband of two years asked,
"Would you like a place in the sun?"

"A place in Florida would be nice," I said,
"I'd really had enough of the cold.
I'd love to see more of our country
before we get too old."

We came down in the fifties before
Martin, Disney, or I-4
Our first son was Joey
Then we had four more.

We lived in south Orlando
and built a house near the Springs
We drove back and forth on Hwy. 441
With traffic and stress that it brings.

When I-4 was finally finished
It cut our travel time in half,
Instead of getting moody
When we arrived we could still laugh.

I just don't understand
When some people say
They don't like I-4
and they go the long way.

The long way they can go
I'll jump on I-4,
I like faster travel and
I'll be there before.

Wanice Blume

I'M ON FIRE

Fall's almost here
and I'm on fire,
My brain is sizzling
I can't get much higher

I need new clothes
So glad I can make them
Must keep up with the times,
I must not forsake them.

They say everything old
comes back again.
I look at old pictures
and then call my friend.

Should I do knits
or should I do cottons
at the store they are stretchy
are knits really back in?

My friend, Louise says, "Who cares?"
just make what you like
If they laugh at your clothes
Tell them, "TAKE A HIKE."

Janet Sage
South Daytona

PURE JOY

In April for the first time there
In California's Muir Woods,
Deeply breathing in the sacred air

A child of three came running up to me
Speaking a language I did not know
From the land of snow
I asked Mom to translate my question
To that child full of joy:
"Aren't these flowers pretty, right here?"
Mom complied and said he totally agreed —
This boy seeking to share
His reverie with me.

Janet Sage

AH, FLORIDA

Waking up, still half asleep, through mazes of rainbow
       dreams at dawn sense suck in sweet smells of red roses
          in bloom at our window

Palms swaying softly remind us of how we arrived here
       from cold northern climes
          to rest our weary shells

Embraced in the soft,fragrant air and sunshine
       of our new home state -
          ah, Florida!

We fall back on our pillows drenched in lemon- yellow sun,
       feeling the fun of the day coming on,
          to bodysurf with dolphins near our door.

       Paradise for sure

Judy Krum
Sanford

MY NONNA'S FACE

I see the patchwork of a life made rich
By sizzling summer heat and winter cold,
Those irregular shapes of time that stitch
Her memories together into gold.

I feel my nonna's face and touch the art
Of joy and sadness, sympathy and pain.
Her wrinkled face reveals the loving heart
That gave all that she had, with no disdain.

I trace her face from forehead down to chin,
Feeling the thick embroidery of life,
Created by a touch, a word, a grin,
And many hours of laughter and of strife.

My nonna's countenance presents to me
A crazy quilted album guarantee.

Judy Krum

PATIENCE IS AN OLD WOMAN

Patience is an old woman,
Wrinkled and grey,
Secure in her rocking chair.
Geraniums bloom in hanging baskets on the porch,
Welcome mat neatly swept,
Shades drawn to keep out the heat.
She tidies the house for anticipated visitors.
Their footsteps echo in the empty hall.
The iced tea is ready.
"They're just delayed," she whispers.
"It's only two o'clock."
The dusting is done.
Glasses and coasters are set on the table.
"It's only four o'clock."
The geraniums are watered.
The lights are turned on.
"It's just six o'clock."

G. Kyra von Brokoph
Ormond Beach

BONNARD'S WOMAN IN THE RED DRESS

On my birthday
I'll burn the London tower,
Climb down to
Barbarossa's cavernous tomb.
Run bulls across Pamplona's
Hoof worn cobble stones.

I am 92 years old.
Led many secret lives.
Jumped ship at Gibraltar
Danced the pelican step and
Drank dark wine
From Zorba's sun warmed flask.
Sea foamed, storm born, rouge no-ire nights.

Now – I lie beneath the Louvre's
Shadowy stairs,
A tremulous, dream warm silhouette.
Crouched down in dusk dim twilight.

Look here, night watch,
Lend me your lantern!
Blood leeks from the woman's
Red dress
Dripping into my drowsy groin
As she lifts
Her black trimmed parasol to toss
A seed into this
My pomegranate grove.

On this bull brazing, cliff scaling,
Tower torching
Dawning of my birthday.

G. Kyra von Brokoph

TIREE
(Hebrides)

A hand of granite raised in prayer
in service to a sullen god.
A church wall once, today a reverie.
Tomb stones turn eyeless heads
onto a cloud blind sky.

As rocks tossed by a disgruntled fist
listless wait for form and fate.
sheep graze drunk on treeless green
while sandy ribbons undulate
along the island's moody seam.

Plain faced houses shivering
hunch low onto their heels.
Black roofs like Shepard's hats
that brim coarse cloaks
shield from tide and tempest.
Sardonic spec of earth.
Uncolored like a poor man's cloth.
Raw shores of calloused hands,
of shipwrecks and of wind torn yearnings.
A place austere and pure –

Up-swept vestige from my heart.

Mary Lou Peffer
DeLand

GOD

"I saw God and she is black,"
Said the astronaut, when he came back
From the depths of outer space
Where darkness reigns in majestic grace.

I like the metaphor he gave
And relate to the nature of God that way-
God is black as endless space
And female as a warm embrace!

I do not adhere to traditional teachings
Or go along with one man's preachings.
God, to me, is just pure love,
Not some authority figure from above.

The universe is wholly a mystery,
Time and space we cannot see -
But i feel secure and right on track
With the astronaut's musing:
"I saw God and she is black."

Mary Lou Peffer

WHERE DOES MY MEMORY GO?

Where does my memory go
when it leaves me high and dry?
Does it dive down deep in a submarine ship
or charter a jet to Shanghai?
Is it attending a conference with other minds gone astray
Or joining a memory commune and moving far away?

I really do miss it and want it back again,
Especially when seeing a long, long lost friend!
Having her name rush into my brain would be
a star in my crown,
But too often it won't be available,
until out the door I am bound.

I know this is not just an old folk's distress,
For kids also forget things to do,
But I'd really like to know where my memory goes,
So that I could join it too!

Peter Francis
Orlando

A FED BEAR IS A DEAD BEAR

Some bears just moved into the neighborhood
Enticed by an easy meal of garbage
Something has to be done
We can't survive with bears in the neighborhood

Some people just moved into the forest
Enticed by the trees and the river
Something has to be done
We can't survive with people in the forest

Peter Francis

WHILE YOU WERE SLEEPING SOUNDLY

While you were sleeping soundly
In the darkness of your room
While you were sleeping soundly
The clouds obscured the moon

While you were sleeping soundly
The air outside was still
While you were sleeping soundly
Nocturnal hunters killed

While you were sleeping soundly
Time continued on ...
Still, asleep you remained
As if nothing could go wrong

While you were sleeping soundly
No thoughts to cloud your head
While you were sleeping soundly
Something stayed awake instead

Kristine Torgerson
Port Orange

SACRED GROUND

Let the cave paintings speak
Your truth becomes known
Climb the staircase of destiny
Bringing forth the ancient handprints
Your motion hasn't been stopped
What your hand has created is eternal
Can tides erase footprints made in the sand
The land has its' own song
Visual music merges the vastness
Infinite's flesh dance
Reaching a pinnacle on sacred earth
The thread of words sewn thru souls
That journey in her space
A gentle walk under the magnolia
True lasting fragrance carried away to grace others
Atoms sigh
DNA now dandelion seeds flown into space
Gathered in the stardust super nova
Divinity imparts
Beauty evolving with an eternal breath
Recreated by God's exhale of new creation
Ever unfolding
The fragrance of a rose releases again
It's aroma upon the land

Kristine Torgerson

RAVEN'S MOON

Authentic Being, yet unsung
Waiting to be transported to naked self
behind the veil
Come walk with me beneath the raven's moon
My heart is lonely treading this journey alone
Path laid with drumbeat of ancient souls
gathered unto their own
Joys silenced by my singleness
echo in hollowed caverns
Caress a smile upon my heart
Wandering, wayfaring companion
my side is weak carrying mother earth's tears
Stretch forth your arm
forged with strength and courage
Lay your ear on this earth clad spirit
Dance to heartstrings of my song played
on etesian winds
Beckoning you come
Empty you're without the sounding
song of your soul
The ravens cry and blacken the moon

Mary-Ann Westbrook
Ormond by the Sea

WADING IN WINTER

January seas wash over
ninety-eight point six
degree feet curling
toes like they are being
tasered. Foam, icy white
swirls around ankles like
drifting snow.

Sun, tanning faces warms
surf and sand cradling
feet in softness as
Wedgwood skies
melt into eyes.

Like moored dinghies
pelicans silently
bob their greetings.
Shore birds offer
the oceans gossip.
Symphony of crashing
waves and frothing surf
calms chaotic minds.

Mary-Ann Westbrook

RIVER PEACE

The eastern sun dances behind
tall trees as we launch into
places waters.
Sabal Palms, Loblollys and Live Oaks
line luxuriant banks as do clumps
of oyster shells below.
The surface - so still - it is difficult to
see where the water ends and
the forest begins.
Snowy egrets wade carefully as
Great Blue Herons stand silent vigil.
Overhead a Bald Eagle lifts into
the sky as smaller birds
call ahead to warn of our coming.
Our fleet of Crayola kayaks, red,
green, yellow, blue and orange
echo excitement in this world of
quiet nature.
Baptized in these waters they
had been perversely dubbed with
names of epicurean delight - Chili
pepper, Pickle, Green bean, Banana
Blueberry and Cantaloupe.
As we glide through the water
miniature eddies swirl off the
blades of the paddle leaving a
wake of bubbles that mark our
passage.
A gentle breeze causes rip-lets
to form on our pathway that our
sleek ships pierce like an
arrow in slow motion.
In this isolated paradise, beauty
fills our eyes, nature's music
fills our ears and serenity fills
our souls.

Joe Cavanaugh
Ormond Beach

IRISH GENES TALKING IN MY HEAD

My grandfather was unknown to me
He lived only in the stories told
By my father most of them
Now safely lost
Disappeared into the relentless
Rhythmic tides of life today

I will remember always the story
Of his cruel words directed
At my fun loving cousin
Who liked to wear lipstick
Make up and floral print dresses

A true homophobe he
Banished this feminine man
To the darkness outside
Of the safety of the family clan
To die alone without love or support

Last year in the California redwoods
I danced near the campfire with my old friend
Doug freeing myself by
Breaking the genetic bond and
Social contract with my grandfather

Joe Cavanaugh

LOVE SONG

The great plan unfolds

Our role in it
What is it?
In our rooms we come and go
Dreaming of dancing
With Michelangelo

Swept along by the raging electronic
Currents at the speed of the morning light
We pause between thoughts
Watching the cardinal land
Near the Buddha rock

Now we know what is it
The life force is creating again
A poem is being made
Part of the great plan
The muse has made a visit

Lucie M. Winborne
Longwood

AFTER THE READING

I would whisper
if you were here
this
that was born

in the echo of
your muscular voice as you stood,
poet at your pulpit,

casting word nets to your hearers.

Later, on a bank of quiet dark
where we'd bared our feet
in a tea-colored stream,

It rippled like a fish in the moon-water:
I would have cupped it in my hands,
a gift to you.

My bed will not hold me. I sit,
forgetting sleep,

whispering this poem to
you who are absent, your crooked stride
breaking the grass
on the way to your own
templed verse.

Lucie M. Winborne

WE ARE STILL WALKING
 for L.C.T.

The hardest trail we walked
was the rail bed in Savannah
abandoned to all but the promise of snakes—

gray gravel with no grass for our feet,

a canopy of sun leaving just breath to breathe

until water was manna that I poured on my neck,
thinking "Never enough,"

until I walked the floors of a hospice
waxed clean of tread and tears

while the white knife of cancer
carved the flesh from your bones
and the timbres from your voice:

That day I left you wrapped in sheets
and bags of fluid, when all the water in my eyes
would never be enough. I knew then
I'd been wrong, that this path was the hardest.

Yet we are still walking. You stride
across my mind with your resolute tread
and strong back unbent. I can level
the trail of memory as I wish, discarding
bad days like pebbles kicked from dirt. There

my footing is sure and you are still beside me
with your face turned towards the sun,

and we are still walking.

Mitzi Coats
Ormond Beach

ORIGAMI

Horse or dinosaur, he asked,
holding a inch square of white paper
between fingernails ringed with grease.
Eyes lasered in concentration through wiry hair
that strayed over bushy eyebrows
oblivious to shoppers flowing around him
he folded, folded again,
snipped a few cuts with scissors
that he carried in his back pocket.
Working from side to side
he folded again and again
until a long reptilian tail, upright body,
shortened forelegs and snout
emerged in miniature
perfectly formed from years of practice.
Careful, he said,
as he placed his gift in her hand.
It might blow away.

Mitzi Coats

STILL LIFE, TABLE

Replacing the oversized dining set
divorced from the chalet living space
my brother retrieves a roughened slab
teetering on skint legs
that has been tossed to the mountainside
of trash headed for the dump

This man of many talents
perhaps not of lasting intimate collaborations
sands splintered edges
scrapes peeling paint and shellac
layers of grime separating
under hairsoft brush and linseed oil
to reveal what he couldn't know for sure
naturally burnished splitgrain planks
deep bronze yellowed ash
pressed together shaker style

He pegs the tabletop upright
to posts straightened sturdy
partners four chairs
their seats slick as babies' skin from years of wear
into kitchen service
centers
over a slivered scar left unsealed
a plain white bowl with fruit
rainbowed firm ripe

Janet Watson
Wesley Chapel

THE TRAIN TO MEKNES

We are bringing to our Moroccan hosts
a large fish, bought just before
this train left the station. It was caught
by a fisherman at dawn, near a spot where
the Sebou River pours into the Atlantic.
In the foothills of the Atlas Mountains,
seafood is a rare treat. We carry
our fish wrapped in newspaper.
It is so fresh that it has no smell at all.
The family in Meknes will bake it tonight.

A middle-aged European sits across from us
in the train compartment. He is eating
a hard-boiled egg for his breakfast.
Yolky crumbs fall from his lips to his lap,
but he seems not to notice.
A younger couple sits next to him—
a turbaned man and his veiled wife who holds
a hidden infant beneath her head shawl.
Beyond the train carriage window,
a tawny landscape whirls by.

The monotony of the scenery and an early
awakening, no doubt, causes the young mother
to nod off. Her shawl slips down, revealing
a pale breast and the fact that the child
had been nursing before she and he fell asleep.
Her husband, drowsy himself, reaches over
to restore her modesty with a tug of the shawl.
My own sleepy eyes open and close and open again,
creating a train of vignettes, each portraying
how far I am from home but how at home I am.

Janet Watson

SEA-WOMAN

We have lingered in the chambers of the sea
By sea-girls wreathed with seaweed red and brown.
~ T.S. Eliot

Slipping into the spring-fed cold of the inlet,
I was soon approached by my hostess,
who welcomed me to her domain.
Round and motherly, her back shawled
with mossy green, the manatee and I
face-to-faced inches below the surface.
Our connection was almost an embrace
while eel grass tickled our bellies.

She did not shrug away from the strangeness
of my mask and snorkel but captured
my glass-enclosed gaze with her own focused stare
in kindly curiosity. I, in turn, found no oddness
in the rolls of her convoluted countenance,
her need of a shave. Gray granny-whiskers
added to her matriarchal charm.

She touched me with a flipper, and then,
with supple swirl, brushed a velvet pelt
along my hip, an obvious invitation
to join her in play. And so we played,
I more clumsily than she, who rolled and begged
for tummy-rubs. Time stood still for our encounter,
neither of us wishing to leave until the chill
shivered my resolve and sent me back to our boat.

Drawn into her water-world for that little while,
I belonged again to the place from which
we all come. The sea-woman recognized
and accepted me. I was a member of the family
who had been lost on land for many years.

This poem won 1st place,
2013 NFSPS WyoPoets Award, published in 2013 **Encore**

Holly Mandelkern
Winter Park

MR. SUGIHARA'S EYES

Through the window Mr. Sugihara spies
a sea of pleading eyes behind the gate;
he sees their lives rest solely in his hands.
The Japanese government first denies
their pleas; escape for these will come too late
unless they leave at once for foreign lands.

To Curacao, the Dutch open their doors;
for Jews in Kovno, the world's a spinning wheel,
rotating them to Vladivostok, then Japan,
needing visas to depart for distant shores.
Thrice Mr. Sugihara wires appeal;
thrice Tokyo halts the motion of his plan.

With furrowed brow and tired, sleepless eyes
the consul weighs which law he will obey;
his hand can save them with his pen—
for transit visa each man in line applies.
He sees there's not a moment to delay,
transfixed by gravity of Jewish men.

Inspired by Mother's roots as Samurai?
His school in Harbin taught "Do much for others,
expect little in return" (his school creed).
Linguistic prowess makes the perfect spy
who sees these men outside the gate as brothers.
Armed with honor, his pen will do the deed.

Steadied by Yukiko, his brave wife,
he signs a passage for each one in line
to Russia's edge, to Kobe, then Shanghai?
For weeks he handwrites visas saving life—
two thousand and one hundred thirty-nine,
the measure of the righteous man's reply.

Holly Mandelkern

L'CHAIM

For Nesse Godin

My eyes will sign a hasty match
that Mama strikes from her wise heart.
A husband quickly she will catch.

Our family had been torn apart,
expelled from home to hostile land.
From nothing, fire is hard to start.

The cling of need predicts a plan
that one of us must race to wed.
We need the brace of a good man.

She chooses me—I can't be led
from spring's remains to winter's year
so Yankel, young, she picks instead.

A glance reveals he seems my peer
of striking looks; I find him fair.
Behalf beholds, she draws him near.

A "yes" from Yankel makes the pair.
At seventeen I sing the pride
of circumstance; they raise my chair,

l'chaim from places where we died.
Mazel—seventy years a bride.

Sarah McClendon
Altamonte Springs

THE MAITLAND COVERED BRIDGE

Somewhere I've seen this covered bridge.
Was it another lifetime? Another planet?
The tendency is to walk quickly through.
And on the other side will be heaven and sunrise.
But love holds me back – a lover's hand? My children's cry?
No, close the view. I'll stay here awhile.
Heaven can wait.

Ruth Titus
Oviedo

SOUL MATES GONE AWRY

Both wore white
on their day of eternal union
The July sun brightly shone
on the pavilion of grass—
a green carpet wedding.

His parents looked strained
and out of place
They made the effort
but knew so little
of the city and social demands.

The bride's aunt from Milton
refused to attend
as it was beneath her
to soil her shoes
with grass stains
for such an occasion.

The groom was adopted
not a Harvard alum
raised by working poor
with ties to the earth
who never denied
to change themselves
into society's wretched farce.

Their home was steeped
in the brisk turn of autumn's air,
and the mud of March.
God's country they called it
Emerson knew it
as well as Harvard—
and he, too, chose the former,
as a serene path to spiritual freedom,
life stripped of society's deceptive mask.

Lynn Schiffhorst
Winter Park

POEM FOR MY MOTHER WHEN SHE IS DEAD

Remember
How we walked along the beach
Last year?

How I walked on ahead of you,
Far, far ahead of you?

You could hardly see me.
You picked out my one bright feature —

A cherry-red jacket —
And knew me by it on the horizon.

Now you have walked far, far ahead of me.
I can hardly see you.

I pick out your one bright feature —
Your heart like a child's red bucket,

I see that still,
Far as you are from me.

Now you do what I did.
Turn —

And run back to me!

Lynn Schiffhorst

ALMOST EVERY MORNING

I wake. I can't get up.
I think: *I can't face this day.*
I get up.

I wash, I eat something,
I think: *I can't face this day.*
I dress,

I open the door,
close it behind me,
unlock the car.
I think: *I can't face this day,*
I start the car.

I get to the office.
Lock up the car.
Walk toward the door
Of the building.
I think: *I can't face this day.*

And then,

Under my right foot,
the invisible, glowing step
comes up.

It carries me into the day.

Al Hubbs
Orlando

PERSISTENCE

When I am low
 and things are tough
When I believe
 I've had enough

When I can't see
 a brighter day
When nothing seems
 to go my way

When bills are due
 and money's gone
When I've no will
 to carry on

When I've lost my
 strength and power
When I must face
 my darkest hour

I look deep inside
 to find true grit
And say to hell with it
 I quit

Al Hubbs

SASKATCHEWAN

It's time I feel to go home again
To the wide open land and the sky
To the hum of a summer's day
Watching a meadowlark fly
And the sun's heat and the bird's song
And the wheat fields in motion
Mark the unseen path of the wind
On this endless prairie ocean

It's time I feel to go home again
To walk long hills by the river
Where Sumach and the Willow grow
And the pale green Aspen quiver
To hear across a still dear lake
The haunting cry of a loon
Or the howl of an errant wolf
On the night of a Hunter's Moon

It's time I feel to go home again
And the call is so crystal clear
From city and town, from field or farm
This sweet music to my ear
Awakens sleeping memories
In this far-flung absentee
It's a great land this west land
And its spirit lives in me

Russ Golata
Greater Orlando

SO, IT BEGINS

You peek at me
A shard of light over the horizon
A passing glimpse of your curves
Blended with wanton anticipation
The world shifts into light
Melting the morning dew
Glistening like the sweat of lovers
Moving to the music of birds
One chirp slowly transforms
Into a wave of moving sounds
The din becomes so loud
Yet all vision becomes clear
Like a sinner at a tent revival
Hallelujah Namaste a new day

Russ Golata

FIRST FLIGHT

Every day the sun says, "Good Morning,"
All the birds seem to sing out your intentions.
This new found freedom comes without warning,
With no fixed place of your destination.

Keep all your senses open to new things,
Let the spirit of the sky lead your way.
No limit to what this fine day may bring,
Soaring over this world in disarray.

Look beyond the realm of where you are now.
Respect the fact that everything is alive.
The world opens like a blooming flower,
A wonderful peace in your heart arises.

It takes faith for a baby bird to fly,
Spread your wings my friends, and arrive.

Sophia DuRose
Kissimmee

REPEAT ME

People say that words lose their meaning meaning meaning
If you repeat them enough.
Sorry only goes so far
And if you keep leaving the scar
Eventually it will refuse to heal.
People say that words word words lose their meaning,
If you repeat them enough.
Sometimes I stay up at night
Staring at the broken galaxies
Which remind me of my family
And wonder does that same principle apply to people?
If I play my father father father
On a loop
Do his insults lose their sting?
Cowering under a blanket can erase so much fear
Until he gets up again shouting shouting shouting
In your ear.
Can my rock candy fortress be as sweet as his eyes?
Can my concrete slab of a brain brain brain
Be as rigid as his ways?
I keep repeating-peating-peating
What he says and it still hurts.
I swear people say that if you repeat a word enough enough
enough times
It will lose its meaning.
What a fragile system
That the repetition of a rhythm
Can dethrone a kingdom built on iteration
And the alliteration of the world
Is not enough to serve its people people people.
They say that if you repeat a line
Enough times
It will lose its meaning.
And that's how I'll be leaving.

Sophia DuRose

DIVE SCAR

If I'm a dive bar
My dad's a regular.
He takes great pleasure
In slapping down tips of guilt
Shortchanging my confidence
And ordering glass after glass of my fragile insecurities.
A ceiling fan of infidelities
Whirls atop his head
Which is fed
Things I've said
In buckets of liquored soul.
There's a chip at the end of my bar.
There since I was young
That scar.
So deep and clean
Yet bubbling with mean
Drinks fall right in.
Nobody wants to sit where I was slit.
I hope I get to send my dad pictures
Of a wedding to which he was not invited.
I hope he thinks
Between half-hearted clinks
Of drinks
"She would have been beautiful if not for that scar."
But he doesn't deserve stitches.

Sean Crawford
Orlando

FOUND MY OUTLET

Wishing I had an outlet to plug my frustrations into
There is just so much I been through
So many ears to hear
But a very few to listen
Is there anyone out there who can understand
If everyone has problems
Then who knows how to solve them
Day by day I'm losing contact with myself
Distancing myself from me
Then being introduced to poetry
I found that I can inhale my frustrations
and exhale my emotions
For this curse that was put on me
I knew there had to be a secret potion
I just didn't know it would be called poetry

Sean Crawford

THE REALIZATION

How could you do such a thing
After I propose to you with a ring
Were there red flags that I overlooked
Maybe those nights I wanted to
take you on a date but you were always booked
Couldn't even use a pen
you always just penciled me in
Then I was erased quick when
you decided to go hang out with your
so called "friend"
Guess I was blinded by the love I had for you
Thought you only were loving me
But come to find out
you were loving a few
Now I'm sitting here debating what I'm going to do
Move on with my life or try one more time
It's hard to think about something else
when you're the only thing on my mind
But I can't see myself going through this pain again
And just to think everything I was doing for you
You were doing to your "friend"
All this time I thought you were too good to be true
Come to find out
I was just too good for you

Alea Plumley
Port Orange

WOMEN OF THE NIGHT

Hints of ashen silk breathe night's thick air
Encircles the opening of their hearts
Hands rest upon crude stone altar
Upturned faces bathed in moon's glare
Goddesses welcome night's awakening

Prayers extending to heaven
From lips of crimson moist
Soliciting the Universe to intervene
As they wait patiently to receive
Healing of their hearts' sorrow

Praying for peace upon this land
Imploring Spirit to assist
Wars have got to end
They cry
       Tormented souls
              Too many have died

Women of the night
Gather on evening's fall
Requesting the Gods' join them
To tear down hatred's wall

Wars are not the answer
Their hearts ache to scream
They pray quietly
Within their haunted dream

Another night will find them
At the altar's cold stone base
Voices murmuring prayers
For tortured souls to find love's grace

Alea Plumley

STAGES

Part I

Wanton women desire companionship
    If only for an hour
As lonely men seek escape from torn hearts
Too shattered to piece together
    Wounds raw
        Scarred over by years of denial
Looking to heal their inner destitute with a moment of lust
Inner peace escapes their reach

Part II

Yawning within rests the child
Cuts so profound they need to be healed
Bandages newly ripped away
As the postulant wound clears
    The child's broken dreams
Now, caressed begins to gently mend the inner disruption
The adult heart beats sweetly
As forgiveness is reached
    For themselves and the perceived hurt laid upon them
Life begins again as they open to allow peace
Loving tenderness covers the unwrapped gash
A precious scab fashioned to remind them
    They must release their past

Sonja Jean Craig
Altamonte Springs

MOMENTARY INSIGHT

Facing life
Looking it in the eye
Absorb the strife
Feel the high

Sonja Jean Craig

THAT ART OF BEING

Looking Life in the Eye

Will I need sunglasses?

Choosing to participate
Requires filters
From the bright light of beingness

In mainstay work-a-day world
I live
Within multidimensional awareness
I soar

From inner and outer perceptions
Third eye beams

From the playground of the mind
Seeing is being

And being is all there is ...

Barto Smith
Eustis

SLEEP ALL THINGS OF BEAUTY

sleep all things of beauty
no man will disturb you
no man can disturb you
let through you are all that there was
are all that there is
and few as the sun moon and stars knew it
who had you asked if not them?
sleep all things of beauty
no man can disturb you
no man will disturb you
you let them be as is beauty's way
and keepsake the what they remember you by
and that is enough yes
that is enough
the sun moon and stars knew it
who had you asked if not them?
beauty is memory and memory must sleep
so sleep all things of beauty
no man will disturb you
no man can disturb you
awake, they are only the day
dreaming the night
passed through your sieve like seeing from sight –

Barto Smith

JUST LIKE TODAY

Just like today, so it was then,
leaves were green, and heavens, blue.
This, all because young fools in love splattered air
with sighs and songs – things they'd recall having seen—
only because leaves were blue, heavens green.

Chaz Yorick
Orlando Area

THE TRUTH

The truth will set you free.
So it must have been the truth
that set my grandfather's dog free.
Free. . . for about 23 seconds.
The truth is dogs chase cars.
The truth is front doors are for safety.
The truth is screen doors are temptation.
Freedom within view.
You can smell the excitement as the screen door lets the
breezes in to tickle your sensitive K-9 nose.
"Ruh Roh, I smell Rexcitement!"
A screen door is only as good as the most careless grandchild.
My little brother couldn't reach the latch any better than my
grandfather's loyal friend;
A friend who had been watching me open the door as intently
as eating at the dinner table.
The food that dropped from the table proved that I was the
one to watch.
I was the bringer of truth.
I was the bringer of freedom.
The truth of free table scraps.
The truth of free open spaces.
Freedom to chase cars.
Freedom to catch cars.
23 seconds of freedom,
Ending in the truth of car meets dog.
The truth will set you free.
Free to run the skies where cars aren't free to run,
And the clouds are easy to catch.

Chaz Yorick

68 DEGREES

Before the splash hit the rocky edges of the spring,
I knew this was a bad idea.
My body convulsed in shock trying to hold my breath.
One hand holding my nose to keep the air in my lungs,
The other holding around my lungs to keep the heat my body
knows.
Soon the current takes me away.
Throwing me against the rocks.
Each rock seems bigger than the one before.
Bruises will decorate my body like tattoos.
The jagged edged rocks will scrape lines connecting the bruises
like permanent marker scribbling out tattoos.
Beyond the initial rocks, I finally get on my tube and float
down the springs on a beautiful summer day.
Nothing can spoil my day
Not even noisy children.
Not even horseflies.
Not even the initial pain of jumping in at the cold source
of the spring.

Debra Wilk
Sanford

MATING WALTZ
for Dorothy Parker

The things I didn't know
Could make a smart girl crazy
It's easy not to grow
When it's wiser being lazy

The men I could outdo
Were less inclined to stay
You beat them all at chess
Then don't get asked to play

A simple thought it's true
I was better then at losing
And the men were more than few
But all of simple choosing

An easy bunch to lose
I'd beat them till they'd leave
Now I've more of less to choose
And hardly time to grieve

Debra Wilk

PAWN SHOP

Baby on her hip
She pleads her case
Tells the man she's on empty
But she's talking to the diamond
He points
No exceptions says the sign
Beneath the clock
She fists her receipt
Into her small change purse
Cursing
While the man up next
Signs off on his tools
Picks up the pen chained to the counter
The words wishful thinking invisibly written
On its well worn shaft
Returns another payday short
Lines up behind the junkie
Bony arms holding God only knows whose stuff
While the man without his tools
Hopes for a better week
Eighteen bills on the sixty owed
Buys another month
Another month ninety six will buy them back
Another month
Feeding nuts to that fat ass squirrel

Ann Favreau
Venice

CLOUDED VISION

I stand in the lobby with coffee in hand,
Vision clouded by salve in my eye,
Lost in thoughts of probing blue lights.
The eye doctor visit is over.

As movement jogs my reverie,
I glance and see the crooked young man.
His flailing arms and jagged walk
Announce his presence here.

Retreating to my private space,
I purposely avoid his eyes.
Indifference spans the pity place.
Three steps and clouded vision
Separate our lives.

His mother comes with coffee steaming.
"Hello," she says to my stoic face.
"Hello," I guiltily reply.
The young man mutters a garbled word
And propels himself away.

I throw away the coffee cup,
The salve still clouds my eye,
While I embrace a second look
That helps me see life clearly.

That young man is a child of God
Trapped in a blemished body.
I wished I'd spied the soul inside
And said hello to him.

Ann Favreau

GAMES OF LIFE

I hopscotched through childhood tossing a flat stone at
prejudice.
Tiptoed though teenage years with the timidity of a bench
warmer.
Volleyed my way through college with a strong serve that
scored a career.
Hit a home run with a happy marriage
rounding the bases four times to win the parent series.
Dodged disease in middle age with an eye on the ball
of survival.
Ran strategy plays on the chess board of business.
Ping ponged across the world keeping score of my experiences.
Jumped over the hurdles of age to carry the baton
to the finish line.

Cecilia Chard
Orlando

WHEN WE WERE EIGHTEEN

I wouldn't want to be
more than I was with you.
I was muffled mayhem,
while you were the glitz
of a disco ball in an empty room.
I would play dead
to hear your laughter.
We filled ourselves with days
of sugar induced blackouts,
piles of cookies and shots of vodka,
ripping our sides open
and sewing ourselves into one.
Ribs rubbing against ribs, and we
threw away the soggy remnants
of licked cupcakes
unwanted.
In our foggy delusions,
we grew old and older
living years in a day.
We traveled to Bombay and Prague,
never leaving our island bed,
picking out constellations
through the stippled ceiling.
I wrote piles of poems
that you set on fire,
and we listened to my stanzas
burn.

Cecilia Chard

EXPOSURE

The air was cold the morning you shot me.
Sun glinted off the lens into my eyes
as I sat so stiff before your Kodak,
wondering what you were hungry to catch.
My body is a landscape you will take.
You call me your sweet muse, and for seconds
I believe you. In your gaze I'm colorless,
black and white and silver on glass. I am
acid washes in dark darkrooms. I am
your subject now, fruit in bowl on a table,
still.

Anton Kozel
Orlando

BETWEEN GENESIS AND APOCALYPSE

Revolution will kill us
Because death is evolution
Now comes a new generation
For whom the door we open
Of people without frustrations
Without discomforts
With visions of preserving what was cultivated
With our missionaries dressed in ante and post meridiem
of long walks and battles
Why don't you let the sunshine in?
Revolution will kill us, and it is our natural selection

Anton Kozel

A FRIENDLY PACT WITH DEATH (UNFINISHED SOLILOQUY)

The linen of your love,
like a grandmother nobody wants to visit,
lulls me when abruptly awakened. I hear your song,
and know the notes it's always brought.
Like playing a violin, and strumming on strings
audible to the soul,
you smiled when the lights were dim.
To hush ... I learned that from you, and am eternally grateful.

My dearest friend, we will go to the lights, and the shadows,
where each one will be in utmost harmony.
And like petals that will fall, I'll be reminded of our romance.
Death, you will watch me when I'm unknowing of your vicinity.
Meanwhile, I will be looking at the colors that I've ignored
all along.
The things I never wrote or said to you, will be revealed when
I'm embraced by the soil, and am back
in your often seemingly distant arms.

Carlton Johnson
Winter Park

ANTYESTI

Tweets & chirps
of wood burning in a pyre —
flames formed feathers.
Wood, green, whines, and hisses
as if speaking words from *moshka*
and another time when you,
wearing your hair in a bun
came undone with laughter and smiles.
Now after the flames settle to smoldering ash
and bone. No longer porcelain white.
The bones gathered in an old silk sari
are carried along with fragile memories
to the river's edges. I trudge with leather sandals
to the Ganges there throwing in
femur, tibia, and phalanges, there to rest
on the bottom of the river — waiting for the fishes
and Lord Vishnu to put them to good use
again.

Carlton Johnson

A (VERY) GOOD YEAR

Oak and pine, closely hewn
sacrificed into planks
flanking the long dark field

Wooden planking forming
right and true angles. Planks
of oak and pine transformed.
One after each other.
Spikes making right
the winds and angles

One by one, cast asunder
under a steel eye of sun.
one hundred open coffins lie.
Lids welcoming, inviting,
those bereft of life.

Long furrows along a shallow,
green pasture and gentle brook—
a living home for these boxes.
The boxes once planted
supplant moist earth from birth
the returning become enduring.

Harp
Orlando

DANGEROUS MUSE

My pragmatic life attempting to take
All alliteration from me,
Leaving an empty shell,
Words and voices stumbling,
Falling into one another,
Without rhyme.
Meaningless word salad,
Trapped inside gray days,
Old mounded, bloated flesh.

Edges of words begin to decay,
In my body lobster-pot,
"L" and "T" and "P" tilting,
Bumping poor "S" and "O,"
Who never had much
Stability anyway.
Lettuce brown, slimy,
Everything drips,
Noxious gasses,
Unable to escape,
Through body apertures.

Bloat continues,
Until sensitive skin stretches,
Fissures replace cells,
Elbow and knee seams,
Let me continue my peace,
The usual routines of life,
But without doubt or surprise,
Returns my dangerous muse.

Harp

DESPAIR

Don't you just
Love despair,
How it cloaks
Itself in multi-colored robes
Of ennui,
Lethargy and
That old life of the party,
Brooding.

Estelle Lipp
Winter Springs

LIKE THE POT

The fire is lit,
steam builds.

Bodies move on the floor,
sliding, gliding,
 finding the groove
of music and flesh
giving way to raw emotions.
Unseen ghostly steam
moving energy,
creates heat,
peaking, near explosion.

Fire withdrawn,
music stops.

Bodies cool
like the pot
moved from the stove.

Estelle Lipp

LIKE CLAY

Like a ball of clay, we begin.
Wet, unformed and malleable,
awaiting unknown forces
that will mold us.

Deft hands work magic,
knowing where to apply pressure,
knowing when to be gentle.
Shape emerges,
at times irregular, often beautiful.

That which outlasts the others
is not hurried,
need not be exquisite,
but must be able to withstand the heat of fire
in order to shine.

Doug D'Elia
Orlando

LITTLE WARNING

When I was a boy
I was bitten by
a German Shepherd.

He came up fast
and silent. I only
heard his growl seconds
before he bit into me.

It was like that for my
friend Danny, too.
He only heard the
screech of tires just
before the car hit him.

And my cousin
Ray heard the click
of the land mine,
that took off both his
legs, having only a brief
second to think, Oh, no!

I wonder how the world
ends. Will there be a growl,
a bite, a click of a warning.
Just enough time to give thanks
or contemplate a comforting thought,
"I'm on my way home now, God."
Or maybe we don't get
the little warning, just some
big-bang swoosh that heaves
our souls back out among the stars?

Doug D'Elia

TOMBSTONE BLUES

Mom insists on living
next to the graveyard
where my brother is buried,
to lay fresh flowers
on him after dinner
and arrange little toys
on his stone, talk to him
like he's sitting here
at dinner waiting
for the meatloaf
to reach his side of the table.

It's been three years since
Khe San, since they
brought him home
in the metal box
and the Notification Officers
came knocking on our door.
It's been two years
since the war ended,
and one year since Dad left,
a lifetime since I opened
the letter approving my
student deferment.

I can see the cemetery from
my bedroom window.
It used to bother me.
I used to have trouble sleeping,
but I've grown used to seeing
him sitting there in his dress uniform
looking up at my window,
tossing pebbles into the darkness
his eyes scanning the void between us,
his face showing confusion and desire
while I sit at the window with my guitar
dodging pebbles and singing the
"Tombstone Blues."

Emily Sujka
Winter Park

CORONARY ODYSSEY

Slide down my valve,
Into a pile of flowers,
Where what lives blossoms and blooms,
And only knows summer showers.
Sweat is rain,
Tears are streams,
With banks cheerily overflowing,
Bursting at their seams.

Discard delight,
Forget sorrow,
Only solace, rest 'til morrow.

Emily Sujka

DEAR 4 AM

Yes, we meet again.
Sobering up for the sun to rise,
Still hours till she
Reluctantly opens her eyes.

Alison Nissen
Lakeland

A BEAUTIFUL BOY

Night bird sings
Blackness looms
Memories bleak
Moon is doom

Love adrift
No home to call
Romance astounds
Heavens fall

God stands firm
At the gates
His magnificence
Trusting fate

Future dark
But bleak it's not
Love's the place
Time forgot

Encompass life
Stars and joy
It's all about
A beautiful boy

Alison Nissen

WANTING MORE

floating, falling
twisting, turning
singing, sailing
hold on tight
to each other, through the sky we swim
at the speed of light

David Axelrod
Daytona Beach

STORIES AND POEMS

It was half light over
streets and sea when I
was brought home,
passed the dog days
but still quite hot
in late July. My
mother wanted me
though an early
fall on icy stairs
suggested otherwise.
My only brother
greeted me with
a murderous stare.
I swear, I still feel
his hands grasping
my throat, his
squinting eyes.
Choked babies
cannot cry. Perhaps
that is why I am
a poet. My father
said he loved us both
but favored his first son —
a story of mythical
proportions.

David Axelrod

DEAR MARY-ANN
 (my friend who says my poems are so sad)

Because I judge myself
I stand accused, tried,
condemned by my own
judge and jury. Because
I trap myself, I am caught,
caged, denied release by
me, the cagey trapper.
Because I choke myself
I gasp, utter strangled
cries, see my bulging
eyes in the mirror of
my strangler. Because
I need to love, I feel
denied, ignored, unable
to love myself without
reprisals. Because I
know these things,
I'm ignorant, unable
to appeal, go free,
breathe deeply, or feel
the warmth of love.
Because I say these
things, you say it's
sad, pitiable, unfortunate
but art is life made finer.
I find a pleasing symmetry
in this explanatory letter.

Robyn Weinbaum
Kissimmee

ANY ROAD WILL GET YOU THERE

Which way you going?
Me, I'm jess heading that-a-ways
Don't matter it far gone
How far all the same
When you puttin one foot after another after another
after another
Oh, I'm fine, I am, real fine now
I got my skin back on, some muscles and flesh
after being bones and nerves for longer than you been
alive, yes ma'am, I was
Seeing the world like them old tintypes or a negative-
you know what that is?
It's a photo but everything is reversed.
They don't make that film, anymore, do they?
VCR tapes, 35 mm, 8 tracks, those itty 110 cartridges
all unraveling now useless technology, world moved
and left it behind
I got left, too. I got left behind, no rapture done it,
nothing like that
I just got left behind.
When I woke up, I figured it was my time to walk and
here I am today and gone manana
Cause if you ain't sure where you going don't matter
how long
or how you get there long as you keep moving
Today, right now, it ain't raining and it ain't too hot
but later, if I'm lucky, my definition of lucky that is,
sunshower to clean me off and maybe a nice shade tree.
I got me a new book and a hat and I'm jess fine.
I'll read a few more chapters or watch the traffic and

▶

Robyn Weinbaum

ANY ROAD WILL GET YOU THERE

(*Continued*)

the trains rushing off to
Important Big Times
Thank you for asking, I'll get there somewhere and it'll be
warm and safe
and my belly will be fulled up
I'll be fine, thank you kindly.
I'll be fine.

Andrea Bateman
Maitland

AT TWILIGHT'S FALL, THE BELLS TOLL

For all the woe this land saw
Before and after the peace it has known,

A peace so gentle it warmed the soul
And blew a breeze,
Lullabying all children of an age,
And land where soldiers fell on poppies red
And children's hands bouquets held, sang songs
Of summer peace as winter never comes,

No intruders broke the sound, a faint bugle in the
distance
Mourns the souls yet to come, for the peace it has known
is as far
As a child's humming a song — lullaby of rest. Of babies
born anew

Volanta Peng
Winter Park

ON DEATH AND DANCING

When my grandmother dies, she is dancing.

Her hair is a sheet of black light.
She moves,
only confined by self-doubt.

She falls and flits away from men's arms,
a bee unsatisfied, finding flowers
in her own steps.

It is night.
Her shoes are stars.

When my grandmother dies, this is my gift to her.

I forget about her peppered insults.
I forget about my mother crying when she remembered
how she wouldn't answer her calls because she thought
we weren't giving her
money out of greed;
the red top in my bag
felt like a thousand missed calls and I had no tissues.
I forget about my grandfather's obvious discomfort as he
sits
on the other side of the couch, waiting for her
to need something from him.
I forget about her cruelty she thought was kindness.
I forget her.

Instead,
she is twirling on her constellation feet,

on into the night.

Nancy Hauptle MacInnis
Cocoa

HOT PINK BALLOONS

Hot pink, balloons on the horizon
framed by majestic verdant palms
on a cushion of flowing silver
ever changing, dances my limbs
alive into bright blue day

Words rise to meet me, desire
to praise, thank Thee, for this
friend, that friend, faithful to no
end, who stay positive through
the spoken, unspeakable negative

Delectable blessing of deliciousness spread
across the table, succulent salt or sweet
bread, butter, meat, fruit and legumes to
eat, drinks to clink in celebration, share with
hearts, souls who love, who care

Looking into the children's eyes, hear
the music of their voices finesse and
prance upon the air, the overwhelming
beauty there, captures one in a hold
of hope, of happiness eternal

Fantasizing about you, the erotic
things we do, the ecstasy of our memory
replay of time together, planning within
provident weather, surprises for our bodies
entwined in this tappin' tango

Saying good bye only when you're ready
allow yourself to cry 'cause it hurts sometimes
steady in the peace that comes with that release
laugh out loud the rising joy 'cause you can't help it
living this, giving into this, exultant life

Nancy Hauptle MacInnis

TO BE A MOTHER

I know of my ability
to be a mother when
first thing I hear in the
morning is "I love you Mommy"

I know how well I dance
as "Mommy" when my teenager
shoots me an air kiss and still
calls me by that name

I know what love my children have
for me when they come again
and again asking mommy about this
requesting that

I know what kind of mother I am
even when my children turn me
away, speak a hurtful word or
two and I say "I love you" anyway

Joan Hartwig
New Smyrna Beach

CHAIN OF BEING

Humility is the hardest thing

For humans to learn.

The natural world is full of

Magic far beyond

Our comprehension.

Where we place in the

Chain of being

Is far lower than

Our minds admit.

Joan Hartwig

DANCING WITH THE MIND

When we try to sleep,
Try to act, and fail,
We dance with the mind.

It fascinates:
Distorts, enhances, creates.
How can we not respect it?

Who puts on the top hat, the spats?
Where's the Fred Astaire
To meet our mind's dance?

Life waits at the door.
The mind bows,
Accepts its daily ritual.

When we're alone at night,
Ready to quit our tasks,
The mind retaliates and says,
"Let's dance."

Margaret Childs Westmoreland
Sanford

FIRE IN THE NIGHT

Five wands
One for each
Blade that flashes
Out from the night.
A hand of flames
With whorls on each tip
That swirls and twirls around the edge
Trying for oblivion.
Only to grab and snap
Back again,
Where caution wants
One more second more
Only to begin again
The fire in the night.

Margaret Childs Westmoreland

THE ICEBERG TOWERS

The heart becomes an iceberg
In the death of Winter.
It stands still, erect, unblemished
Where rock bottom hits down
Way below the tip of the top.
It wallows in water that surround,
Peaking up against it shores.
It never wears down,
Only building, adding more layers
To its everlasting structure.
The Heart has grown strong
And will not cease to love,
Though its need may never be met.
Foundations are strong a
When the iceberg towers.

Joe Rosier
Lake Mary

CENTRAL PARK WINTER
Central Park, February 18, 2003

If I had lived
in the city
I would have
played hooky.

I would have
grabbed a sled
and went to the park

I would have
slid down the hills
had a snowball fight
with the young boys
and rolled in the snow.

I would have fed the squirrels
some bread
and watch the birds jump about.

Later in the day
I would walk to the
Central Park Zoo Cafe
and have a cup of
hot chocolate
to finish it off

Then I would
walk in the snow
and tarry on the way
and I'd forget
that I was too old to play.

Joe Rosier

WRITE WHERE YOU ARE

you don't have to go
off on a retreat
or find a cabin
in the woods

you can write
anywhere
you can create
at any time

you have a mind
God gave you the
ability
so use it

don't tell me
you "can't"
don't make
any excuses

just do it
and show me
the results.

KJ Roby
Orlando

CHARLEY, 2004
after Mary Oliver

The winds arrived like no
wind I'd previously experienced.
Non-flying squirrels flew.
My son stood angled, laughing,
as it flattened his clothing,
parted his hair. Afterwards, the neighbors
emerged carefully,
stepping over limbs, climbing around
downed power lines, calling to each
other – sharing stories over
grilled meats in a communal meal
as they hurried to cook all that thawed.
Men roamed the streets like
Hollywood monsters, waving
their gas-powered chainsaws, and clearing
driveways. We waved
to trashmen, to linemen
from far away states, and for once
didn't complain when
the yardmen powered up their
noisy blowers. The story took over our lives;
we forgot anniversaries
and television, bills and homework.
We wondered why we'd never shared a meal
with that family next-door, and promised
to continue the trend. We conserved
our cash, restricted our driving, and
sat on our porches to capture
a breeze, nodding to explorers
counting houses under trees. But then
the power came on, and
we went back inside.

Originally published in
Pif Magazine, October 1st, 2014.

KJ Roby

HIDDEN IN THE BLUE RIDGE

Even now, forty or thirty years later,
I remember the heat of waking up alone.

Southern Living,
hidden
in the Blue Ridge,
without fear of retribution, punishment.

Between the shower-shoes
and the black-and-blue OP one-piece bathing-suit with
matching shorts
falls the guilt.

A toast to love and laughter and happiness ever after.

Perhaps the fear
did not dare drive past your house;
perhaps the fear
of unbridled passion, sunlight,
and the glory, the glory of the Lord.

Not your Mother's
green lawns (pre-Disney manicured),
blood-red nail polish,
"Barely There" pantyhose,
but I was afraid. I was afraid

Do you remember the twenty-first day of September?
Caught in a moment. Two cross streets. Both brick.
I think of the places we might have gone.

Carolyn Shealy Freligh
Winter Park

FACING NOW

Swirling in the gyres
of a Sargasso Sea,
downhearted and lost
in seaweed memories
with no rocks to chuck.
Dreams of past futures
shelved with bygone faith.
Trapped in a charade,
pride-blocked exits,
broken promises,
gone in a whisper.

Life recovered.

Carolyn Shealy Freligh

UNCLOSETED

The world inside a memory
sits quietly, draped in forgotten sighs.
Exploring moments of time
I find the touch that sparked a promise —
ripe-picked strawberries bathed in champagne,
sugar sand and piña coladas,
salty air-scented waves nostalgic,
eyes that danced, blue, in the clouds,
a voice once sure and strong, silenced.
Each memory a comforting pillow,
eases warm loss in winter's stretch.
Recall the first formed kiss
quaffed to lusty brews drunk with delight,
egg hunts and shelling by the sea,
each thought bright as gulls in sun flight,
shadowing love.
Linen dreams stored on shelves of hope
vie for space with wishes
tangled in mangrove confusion.
Dusty boxes, like stacking blocks,
await an opening
to contents caressed, recalled, relived,
and folded into
the space of future memory —
inventory of other rains.

Evelyn Hoth
Ormond Beach

GHOST

Today I found my pink-flowered blouse
The one worn often because you liked it so
Now it is quite faded
A ghost of my past

I remember your gleeful smile
The bright twinkles in your eyes
Your hearty laughs
Children giggling at your antics
How could I forget?

Hundreds of gleaming red apples
At a country cider mill
Their aroma filling the autumn air
While we sipped their sweet nectar and
Rejoiced in our love

I remember strolling beside the glimmering Atlantic and
Chilly misty walks at the Pacific, your favorite place
Smiling so much my jaws ached
Your gentle hugs and passionate kisses

So many marvelous memories
I can't forget
Thank God
I hope I never do

Evelyn Hoth

MUSIC OF THE MASTERS

Beautiful music plays
The notes joyously rippling
Guiding us
As we sing
The music of the Masters.

Slow and romantic
Then festive and spirited
Andante, allegro, pianissimo or forte,
The music inspires our passions.

We sing melodies of many cultures
Handel, Bach, Gershwin, Mancini, McCartney
And countless others.
Our voices blend in sweet harmony
As our hearts sing along.

Celebrating the music
We feel it soar
Lifting our hearts
In a concert
Singing to our souls.

Frank T Masi
Windermere

LOST

A man is lost; please find him now.
Time's getting short, and night will soon bow.
He strayed off path while we marched on.
And before we knew it, he was gone.

We remember him well, a sturdy young breed.
To laugh and love were his only need.
He joined our ranks and hollowed much ground.
His pick and shovel made a musical sound.

If you but look, he'll be easy too find.
For 'tis you who can see, and he who is blind.
A festering disease beclouded his sight.
He could not find his way through the night.

He wears a frown, a sullen mask.
To live each minute, a grueling task.
He walks with pain, a tortured stride
Bent from a haul with none at his side.

You'll easily see that he bleeds from the heart.
The wound is as fresh as it was from the start.
His eye will tear. Show no surprise.
'Tis painful to have love returned with despise.

And yes, when you meet, give your hand and a nod.
For he's alone now, you see; he's lost his God.

Then bid him return. Say we want him back.
Point out light shining through fearsome black.
Say that his love will always be known.
Only those who don't love die all alone.

Frank T Masi

CHILDREN WITH WRINKLED FACES

The tool of time etches the mask
But takes us only bodily to task
We think experience our childhood erases
But we're only children with wrinkled faces.

We play with toys and then with guns
We fight our fights, all senseless ones
The losers then in mud would lie
Only now it's do or die

From rocking horses to automobiles
From Enfamil to diet meals
From birthday parties to banquet places
Go we children with wrinkled faces

We wean our milk, and then our wine
We draw our strength from a sweeter vine
The nectar then would grow us straight
Now it serves to deteriorate

Forever young, yet always old
Wiser now, or so we're told
Changing some, yet not at all
Marking time till curtain call

Seed and flower are one and the same
Roots are roots, no matter the name
Though we deceive ourselves with silks and laces
We're only children with wrinkled faces.

Gillian Wolfe
Davenport

WELCOME

At it's very, very best
a marriage between
one man and one woman
is a place of nurture and growth.
A place where both are cherished
free to become whole.
A place where life is built
shared together in
respect, blessing and faith.
A sacred place of love
at it's very, very best.
And now, at last, an invitation
extended to all couples
who desire to experience
that sacred place of
love, blessing, faith and life
at its very, very best.
Welcome.

Gillian Wolfe

JANUARY 1ST

A new season of hope
with basic rights restored,
babies born,
resolutions kept,
knees bowed,
and hearts convicted.
Forward into a new year.
Forward into a good year.

Jane Peterson
Winter Springs

CHANCES

She left through the revolving door;
he took the side exit.
They hailed the same cab.
He stepped back
as she stepped in.

In the coffee shop he noticed
the red scarf of a woman
standing in line.
At the theater she glanced at a man
with blueberry colored eyes.

At the airport they rode
the same escalator, Gates 1 to 11.
She Chicago, he LA.
He caught the silk
of her perfume;
she slalomed the camber
of his sweater.

Spring forward, fall back.

At a cocktail party
the clocks unwind.
Perfume, eyes, scarf,
surprise.

If love is a gift from angels,
wrapped in light,
it is also a series of missed chances
awaiting collision,
in a real life.

Jane Peterson

GAPS

There are gaps in our lives
we cannot see or hear;
      they flash freeze the mind,
      stop speech,
      seize the breath.

The agonizing second between
      "I love you"
      and, "I love you, too,"

The mute
      seeing his newborn.

The rogue plane
      dissolving a tower.

Greater gaps —
strands of universe
waving goodbye,
dancing between
      clouds of stars.
Gaps traversing galaxies
to find specimens that are us
      as we go about our daily lives.

And angels whispering through gaps
      saving us from disaster
      with their impossible benedictions.

Gaps confound us,
stop us in our tracks;
square boxes on a round earth,
they are a camera's click
before eternity calls us.

Katie O'Malley
Orlando

HOUSE OF ME

The house has walls built from silence,
Filled with holes and cracks
That ooze abandoned dreams.
Stands alone in fields of memory.
Lights left on elect the pretense of poise.
Attic filled with clutter,
Pile atop pile of joys hidden, swept under the carpet,
Questioning, wondering if any of it's worth it.
My attic head is too heavy for my feeble neck, never free
Of the rummage weighing me down.
Foundation worn away, pieces chipping off, crumbling like my soul,
No longer a strong base that holds up the wooden frames.
My feet too weak to prop up these frail beams; these splintering bones.
The bathroom sinks weep, handles long to be turned,
Floors are flooded with fantasies, slipping between tile cracks
Like water flowing through grated tubs.
Windows are barred, webs hung like garlands,
Sills adorned with thorns.
Blinds not brave enough to face the world; to open my eyes.
Door always latched, the key lost – hidden,
Back gate locked in rust crawling up fence posts that scream warnings.
            Entrance forbidden.
Force doesn't shift these hardened bolts,
As much as I try, they do not unlock.
This house of me that weeps but no one sees;
The outside deceives the eye.
This house of me that neighbors none,
A debt of dues unpaid.
This house of me -
            This house *is* me.
            I'm slowly falling apart.

Katie O'Malley

IDEAL

Stiff, forced smile glued into place on fine porcelain skin,
Rigid nose like clay molded to make breathing demanding,
Glossy blue eyes gleam faintly, blue from concealed tears;
Tears of acid salt that would burn skin if she let them spill.

Glistening golden locks run down her trembling spine,
Teeth almost as pure and white as the girl to whom they
belong.
Lips crimson red like the blood she wishes wouldn't flow;
Heart pumps bittersweet honey through her frail torso.
Oh if perfection had a look, it would be based off her;
Her eyes, her hair, her nose, her cheeks; unrivaled, nonpareil.
But if perfection wasn't an illusion,
People may have seen what was inside,
And this miserable, despondent girl, might still be alive.

Niki Byram
Daytona Beach

A LIFETIME OF HIDING

A lifetime of hiding, all for naught.
You can draw in a deep breath now,
No one, but I, will ever know why;
And you'll never be caught.

You can come out of your shell now.
Your own private hell, it's over,
So, feel comfortable with yourself.

At one time, you asked me to
Be your wife, even as you envisioned
A lifetime lost to condemnation and fear.
Those close to you wouldn't tolerate
Your fascination with me, you calling me dear.

You caved in under their pressure, one year later
You became engaged to, and subsequently
Married another; with everyone thinking you'd
Passed over the hurdle that was me;
Now, you were in the clear.

And, just as I never forgot, nor forgave you;
Somewhere in the back of your mind,
You too, must have thought that one
Day you would have to pay your dues.
Apprehensively, year after year, you waited
For the "Boogey Man" to appear.

And much to your dismay, there came that day!
Your apparition came out of the closet;
Where you had taken it out of your
Heart and put it away; hidden.
I, showing up on your doorstep, for just
A short visit, was unwelcome, unbidden.

Niki Byram

REMEMBER HOW IT WAS

When I came to your door,
And you realized who it was,
Did you feel just
A little bit of tingling,
That old excitement or
Perhaps just a twinge.

And when you realized just
Who it was; was it, you know,
Like the old days,
When just my presence
Or my glance, could make
You come unhinged.

Joseph M. Dunn
Titusville

MT. HOFFMAN
Yosemite

Past the tree line, oxygen is dear
As though the branches' silent
Breath had been sustaining me.
With no more trail, cairns of
Kindness left by earlier travelers
Led to what appeared an anciently
Contended stronghold:
Frost-hewn granite layered
Winter-spring stands in ramparts
Like what the castle-keepers
Made exact with separate stones.

This roofless summit-field—
Far-towered wall, redoubts,
Horrific breaches to the ward,
Seems transplanted from the ruins
That the Empire blended with the British past.

A closer walk among the cornered
Crags frees the vision for the
Valley mountain-garden—
Half-Dome, Sentinel, El Capitan—
More distant, farther below
Than I had thought, enough to seem
Another world's ecstatic closeness,
Like a dream of planets kissing atmospheres

Joseph M. Dunn

SOLILOQUY

The whole damn world is coming to a boil.
Iraq was hatched in Nineteen-thirty-some
as if the Merrie English make a joke
they called Partition—a tuck of border here,
a nip of politics, and now there's ISIS,
a perdition-bound fanatic army.
The Arabs used to rule an age of light
while Europe blundered through its Dark one,
but now the different tribes can't stand each other's
stinking ways—so what is this diplomacy?
And every little state of world affairs,
aggrieved by aggravation, has its say.

Our melting pot is bubbling, too, with race
and immigration in a lousy fuss.
At least the Persians look a lot like us.

Jenni Sujka
Davie

I AM

Tasting the air of another morning,
having seen dawns first blink through my pink window shades.
Adhering to my mother's wishes to come down for breakfast,
naked touch from water for my morning wake-up shower.
Knowing the feeling of my inflating lungs as I breath,
foreseeing dad's French Toast before the smell travels up the
stairs.
Using my arms to beat my brothers, racing down the stairs,
loosing honorably to my sister who gets the first slice.

Jenni Sujka

SECOND MESSAGES

I.
For my love of country music.
Triple chocolate heartbreak pancakes.
My boots and learning gun love.
I could do much better.
You still can't dance.

II.
Always take your keys when you go running.
"Nothing good happens on the beach at night."
Cold spoons and makeup don't work.
Turn your phone off when you're sick.
Stick with final decisions.

III.
Retainers are dentures.
My passion for lifting and Boba Tea.
The strength to move on.
Understanding people don't change.
Listen to your friends and family.

IV.
It's OK to feel good together.
Don't sneak around family.
Avocado and eggs together.
I still don't want to drink.
Hot power yoga.

V.
Couch and chair movie separation.
Frosted Mini Wheat's and Bonehead.
Good can come from sketchy apps.
Some guys will put you first.
S'mores for no reason.

VI.
Morning food is a necessity.
Fit is not mandatory but preferred.
Common ground is helpful.
Being a secret doesn't feel degrading.
Blazing Saddles.

Augustus Sol Invictus
Orlando

BLACK LAKE

What waters once were peaceful
    speed now by the rustling shore.
What air was once warm
    now chills through my jacket
        this untouched skin,
            these grave-longing bones.
February, cold month of lovers
        leaves us loveless,
        leaves me wondering whether
    that night in August was a dream.
No loon cry,
    moon now unceremonial,
        neighbors' chatter &
            passing cars, airplanes,
    the once-quiet branches
        now loudly shaking, mocking –
        and here I sit upon the stone bench
        beside your ghost,
and here I feel like phantom lead
the absence of your hand
when your hand sought mine,
feel like oblivion
the eyes that no longer look
over the lake with me,
like acid
the absence of your head
upon my shoulder,
my loving Circe.
Turn these noises to silence,
    these winds to your breath,
this ghost to flesh & let me feel again
    that warmth of my witch-queen in August.
Ask me again to come to your bed,
    & let us never again have memories.

Hannah Allen
Orlando

A HOLY LAND EXPERIENCE

Reassemble the tower whose bricks have fallen,
Assemble in the building with a crown on it,
Lay stone atop stone, wash them,
Clear the air! Clean the sky!
Rebuild this continuing city,
A nation dried out, stoned,
Replace the tree with one of pines and needles,
Green like our hills,
Red like our sun,

Angela Nguyen (The Forever Alone Truth)
Orlando Area

OPERATION D.E.P.R.E.S.S.I.O.N.

Deep in the dismal darkness, I questioned my existence.
Existence was useless, worthless, or at least, mine was.
Pathetic.
Pathetic waste of space, time and energy, and I was
reminded.
Reminded of everything that was wrong with me
every day.
Every single day, I groaned at a mirror and painted my
smile
Smile, because everything was pointless, and everyone
hated me so.
So tired, the depression drained me, yet at night, I could
not close my eyes.
I heard that the thoughts never go away.
Oh, I was tired, of the depression, most of all, so I gave
up. I was done
No more. I got up, and grip by grip, I began my
ascension from the deep.

"Poetry is the one place where people can speak their original human mind. It is the outlet for people to say in public what is known in private."

~ Allen Ginsberg

Greg Garvis
Groveland

FROM THE MESSIANIC PSALMS

To whoever is reading,
I don't know if you've been in a hurricane,
a tornado, it's rough. You get shaken,
things get thrown—
people are killed by this mess.
See, I do not want it to be me
in there.
Not that person, alive,
a spirit lying dead.
And not for me, but everyone.
I want to be that rock, that protected place
that does not get moved.
In the rain of humanity
I want to be the shield that blocks
the sword,
sword of faceless enemies.
I can do all things, one man said,
with trust in Him.
Terror knows no God, and God knows
no terror.
So what I lose in the storms of life,
and the storms of people, I lose. What I win,
I have already won. It is safe here.
Come, now.
This way, straight on till morning.

Greg Garvis

FOR WILLIAM BLAKE, AND ME

My day is as so;
I run through fields
yelling to my friends, lets go!
One day is calm,
the next irate;
this day joyful,
next, sad, sedate;
this day, good as good enough
next day, mad for hate.
For I wish all days would be as this–
the tigers live low,
the hawks fly high;
as my day goes
and days go by
I wish to live in one,
long brilliant one,
where merry, merry only, is the cry.

Catherine Giordano
Orlando

WHO ARE YOU BECOMING?

Who are you becoming?

My little newt, my little tadpole,
swimming in a sea of unknowns.

Who are you becoming?

My little chrysalis-encased beauty
waiting to burst free into a world of wonders.

Who are you becoming?

My own little bit of amorphous stardust
Metamorphosing into existence.

What are you thinking?
What are you dreaming?
What are you yearning to do?

I know that you will become
the becoming that most becomes you.

My little newt. My little tadpole,
My little chrysalis-encased beauty.

My little darling.

Catherine Giordano

EMBRACING YOUR INNER CRONE

The Druids carved women's life into three:
First, Maiden, nubile sexuality,
Second, Mother, fruition and family,
And last, Crone, wisdom and serenity.

Finally, the time has come to face it.
Denial's cocoon tried to encase it,
But now it's burst free, so don't debase it,
Your inner crone, you must embrace it.

It's true, age brings physical dysfunction
But there is a happy compensation—
The later years do bring gains in wisdom,
Self-acceptance, confidence, liberation.

You have not become, you are becoming.
So many ideas, your brain is humming.
Your life's days, you're not summing.
You now dance to a different drumming.

These are your glory days, lived avidly,
You're discovering creativity,
You indulge in wild spontaneity,
All because you achieved sagacity.

Despite my complaints, my health is still fine.
I keep fit, eat right, toe my doctor's line.
So I plan to be here a good long time—
I think I'll live till one hundred and nine.

Russ Hampel
Winter Springs

TIMELESS

She is art, music and nature.
She is Monet, Van Gough and Renoir.
She strolls the banks of the Seine,
where gentlemen vie for a chance
to paint her portrait,
to write her into poetry. ...
Her beauty rivals the flowers in the market place,
the parade of ladies with parasols in gloved hands,
the sleek boats with white billowed sails on the river.
She is all of this and more
Auburn hair caressed by the wind,
Soft skin tanned by the Parisian sun,
Eyes that blend the colors of the sky and the sea.
She is timeless.

Today she walks through an arboretum
along a great river.
Music plays across a grassy field.
The afternoon sun assumes the role of artist
playfully painting elm trees into long shadows.
She sees the world with her heart,
hides the traces of a difficult life,
notices the little things.
There is no marketplace, but there are flowers.
No parasols or white sails, but a familiar soft breeze.
Has she been here before?
If she has, her beauty has not since diminished.
The only change is her increased capacity to love.
She is art, music and nature.
She is timeless ...

Russ Hampel

DREAM

She is a wonderful dream
and I am vivid dreamer
I try desperately to remain asleep
to extend my time with her
If I awake, I will lose her,
lose her subtle earth essence,
lose her ocean blue eyes, and
the soft contours of her skin.

The rising sun becomes my enemy
My curtains offer no protection
from the yellow rays of light
that slip between the panels.
and wait to flood my yet unopened eyes

I can hold out no longer
I can hold HER no longer
Must awake,
surrendering to the world
outside my sub conscious.
She is gone now,
and her details are dissolving
with every waking minute

I am upset but not discouraged
Tonight I will search for her again,
breathe in her earth essence,
swim in her ocean eyes,
caress the soft contours of her skin
For I am a vivid dreamer
and she is a wonderful dream

Tais Phillips
Orlando Area

9 DASH 5

I sit at my 9 dash 5
Trynna stay alive
When all the while I long to run outside to rid of this
artificial heir

Longing to wake up around 10
Grab a pen
And jot down a few happenings that passed while I was
dreaming

Dreaming about utopias
And thoughts untapped and lands untouched
And words that mean so much
But remain unsaid; dancing around in my head...I have no
chance to write them down

"Thank you for calling ABC Company, how may I help you?"
No. How may I help ME?
I need to break free
But free seems so far away

So I sit in my car during rush hour traffic
On my way to being jerked, I mean..on my way to work
Trynna balance this pen and paper on the steering wheel
Expressing how I feel
About my current state of mind
But now I have a parking space to find
So I solemnly tuck away my paper and my pen
And in 8 hours I can pick it up again
And try to balance it on the steering wheel
To continue to express the way I feel
About my current state of bind

K. Moideen
DeBary

THE NEW FACTORY

The chimney of the new factory
across the street
Vomits white fumes of exhaustion.

Withering souls emerge
through the gate like zombies
wearing loose blue uniforms
precipitated by the sound of the evening siren.

Their faces glow like burning charcoal
in the evening sun
which casts long shadows behind them.

They walk together with staggering steps
weary and drained
with dirt crawling all over their skin
to their little huts scattered across the field.
Footsteps staining pale grass on the path.

Sun sets in the distance
while they drag their lean bodies
through the doors of their huts.
Darkness and loneliness
wait for their arrival.

They sleep alone in their thin beds
covered with warm sheets
dreaming about spring and yellow flowers
and a forgotten wedding ring.

They wake up, rub their pale eyes
and gather their bones from the floor
wait for the next siren
that would blast the neighborhood
before sunrise.

A.J. Huffman
Ormond Beach

FOUR . . .
    after *Leaving Earth*, artist Osnat Tzadok

Three . . .
Two . . .
One. I am
a rocket, reclining in comfort of my own
bed. Blast off rings like an alarm. I ignore
adamant urgings. Eyes closed, elevation
becomes indistinguishable from free-fall.
Floating
dirigible,
my body emulates weightlessness, forgoes
tentacles of commitment. Attachments snap
like tomorrows. I am a star without drama.
This must be what it means to truly fly.

A.J. Huffman

BIBLIOPHILE

The scent of brittle pages fills
my lungs. I am a child again, new wonder
growing with every breath. A tentative turn
of page, eyes scanning for coveted text:
First Edition. A goldmine
of uneven edges. I fold
my mind within posed embrace. Pulling
the vision up to my chin. I am comforted
by context, subtle innuendo, content
inside this imagistic home.

Teresa Edmond-Sargeant
Orlando

SELF-PORTRAIT WITH BIRTHDAYS

As each year goes by,
I wonder
Did I do much with my life?
I graduated from college
Magna cum laude,
Written a poetry book,
Raised a child,
Have written three unpublished novels,
Been through two bad relationships
And spent a week and a half in a hospital.
My birthday is August 27
And I wonder,
"Is this all I have to my existence,
to say that I've
Ached through a lot
And
Achieved a lot?"
Should I have been
A rock star
Or
A reality TV star
Or
A rich witch?
Should I have been a
Somebody
Or a somebody else?

Teresa Edmond-Sargeant

AN EDUCATION IN FAME

God created humans in their own images.
But collagen, beauty salons and ads
Create socially acceptable images
Ugly people could begrudge.
Paper cuts from flipping through tabloids.
Headlines splash across pages.
Libraries lined with tabloids. An education in fame.
Don't expand the mind with books.
Expand it with air.
Swarming with paparazzi,
Money to count from scandal.
Consciences are cleared once bank accounts are stuffed.
Why save up money for Yale or Rutgers
When it could be saved for a Bentley or Dior?
The most important paper is not a B.A. or an M.A.,
But the National Enquirer.
The most important magazine cover to appear on
Is not TIME or Newsweek,
But Star, In-Style and People.
Remember what Andy Warhol once said?
Because I don't.
It doesn't matter anyway.
He's had his 15 minutes.

Rick Mandriota
Orlando

SCHISM

I looked in the mirror
And heard the other guy say
"I'm you and you're me,
Together we can make it clearer
That I let you do as you may,
There's no one else here
No one else who can do that
Except me — You got that
Or do I need to prove it to you?"
Am I crazy? I asked myself,
"No Way," he said.

Rick Mandriota

TRULY RIPPED

During these times
Before I made it big,
I sat in a hallway
Writing down all these words,
Ones which set me free from
The doldrums of life and the
Sour fruit it promised me.
I sat and listened to the
World as it moved, to the
Beggars who stole garbage at night
As if they did not want to be
Shamed by the public light
Perhaps as I do now,
Still sitting in the hallway
Writing what I observe
Instead of getting up and realizing
That if you don't play
You can't win, and though I've
Traded all my sins so that
I may not lose, I still chose
To sit here penning down my thoughts,
Creating my own world, the ones that
Cannot be bought and dream of
The time when all is fine
So that I could just sit around
Drinking wine in a hallway with my dreams.

Shelley Stocksdale
Winter Garden

SANDBAR SANCTUARY

They are letting the lake lie.
They are letting the lake die.
They are telling us the lake is not
a living, breathing entity.
They've pulled the plug,
up grow earth's weeds,
down drains water's sludge.
The lake's crust encircles
a deadly, poison cake.
It's allowed, avowed
to dry browner and browner
dying daily day by May day
under that hot, old Florida sun.

They are cursing: "No one will care."
Every stinking fish will float belly-up
back home, leaving poor birds in wake,
stranded, standing knee-deep on sandbars ...
too many, too tall, newly risen out of sea.

The birds stand lost —
looking for their sinking,
blue, liquid beauty.

> *May 28, 2012*
> *Memorial Day*
> *Remember Lake Apopka?*

*Rainfall, North Shore Restoration (SJRWM), with
restricted, water draw-downs; have returned
Lake Apopka's levels to "near-normal" (2015).

Shelley Stocksdale

PROMISES, PLATITUDES, POLICY ATTITUDES

Malaysian Secretary of State states:
"We will never give up…
we owe it to the families."
Today we are posted 42 aircraft and sea ships
sent from twelve countries who are searching,
scouring , combing the skies, the waters,
the land looking for airplane metal debris;
huge piles of dead bones, bodies, blood.
What will floating funeral pyre show us
poking above cracked wake we ponder,
as we try to fill-in splashed, dark spaces
before our forlorn, flat tv screens?
Fiberglass, fuselage, fuel,
Dixie cups, dinner plates, safety belts,
tiny pillows, tiny blankets, tiny suitcases,
high-heeled shoes, neckties, hats,
magazines, newspapers, maps,
emergency instructions, wine bottles…
all grown water-filled, more than soggy
or drifting, about to be washed-under
graves by ever-rolling, unforgiving waves.
Malaysian military plus airport tracking
had been turned off, stunned we are to hear.
Prime Minister Hussein maintains:
"We have handled the matter
in a transparent way from the beginning."
*Malaysian Airlines Flight MH 370, disappeared
on March 12, 2014 with 239 passengers aboard.

Tamla J. Thomas
Orlando

I HAD A DREAM LAST NIGHT,

you came home
flowers in your hand
you told me
I was the best thing
that walked into your life.

you came home
dinner was waiting
ready for your consumption
lights low, soft music playing
in your honor.

you came home
Bath hot bubbles floating

You came home
I was standing there
with nothing on but
your tie around
my neck

Waiting for you.

Tamla J. Thomas

YESTERDAY

Sitting, thinking, remembering.

What happened to yesterday?

Why, I cannot bring that day back, lost
in time.

What happened to what was?

Deep regret, deep hurt unfulfilled dream
now a shadow gone.

The dream that once was perished, the
subconscious, but a fading memory of wanted to be.

Why does there have to be a yesterday?

Can't everyday be today?

Yesterday has shaped, molded, and
formed me into the being I am today.

Strong, Loved and Admired.

Susan C. Cravotta
Winter Garden

OH, WINTER CHILL

Oh, winter chill, why come you here
      to turn the earth's green blanket brown,
While seeds and petals gently fall,
      from blossomed heads now pointing down?

And mighty trees who still stand tall
      expose varied states of undress,
Green leaves turned brown silently fell,
      to reveal the abandoned nests.

The, birdsong choir long has flown
      to warmer climates, now their home,
And new birds gracefully alight,
      fleeing the cold from whence they've come.

The North finds rain turned crystal white,
      snowmen and snow forts fast appear;
Pond water hard on which to skate,
      for young and old who have no fear.

Oh winter chill, when your time's passed,
      and seeds once dropped will start to bloom,
I'll glory in the warmer days,
      so thankful Florida's my home.

Susan C. Cravotta

THE PEN

The pen lay there upon the desk,
      how silently it slept.
No word or thought had issued forth,
      it lay there still, inept.

Then one day pen was lifted up,
      and felt its owner's hand.
It knew such joy such happiness,
      and waited the command.

Pen lingered, perched, to skate along,
      the pure unprinted page,
But nothing happened, not one stroke,
      to form a new image.

Pen thought, dear, owner, can't you see,
      thoughts, feelings all around?
Grab all that hover in your mind,
      and heart, for they abound.

Enlightened, owner channeled thoughts,
      perused them one by one
Then, by command, pen skated fast,
      until its task was done.

Bryan Tracy
Orlando

LIFE IS FUNNY

You can do everything right,
And still go to bed with an empty stomach at night.
Sometimes I think we're being punished
for actions committed in a past life.
I see good people suffering,
With no end in sight,
Victims of consequences,
Some not seeing the light,
I've been told that life on earth is hell,
The burning of a desperate soul,
Makes up for not seeing the fire in sight.
Hopes that flames distinguish,
Burning desires that are nonexistent.
The feeling of I can't win seems to be the attitude.
If you're alive you're winning,
So somebody's got you fooled.
I refuse to believe that its human nature to be
subservient
Natural born leaders are born everyday

Steve Spellane (aka WolfSong)
Orlando

With apologies to Lowell S Alexander

LANGFORD PARK

Dappled sunlight filtered by moss hung trees
With quiet chirp birds call to me
Wooden bridge across small slow brook
Pause here now to watch and look

Flowers still bloom at end of season
They follow not calendar rhyme or reason
Squirrels scurrying at a frantic pace
Chasing one another in a dizzying race

A lizard travels across my path
Pause and look, then run real fast
A peaceful day with clear blue sky
A hawk now calls with a nine chorus cry

Late afternoon sun shines from west
As homeless gather under pavilions to rest
They build small wood fires in empty grill
To cook a meal, and banish evening chill

Stand and stretch, put down my poem
Walk to the car and then travel home
Light slowly ending, approaching dark
A peaceful day in Langford park.

Susan Groves Peyton
Orlando

ODE TO A BRIGHT PURPLE TRIKE

When I am old and sassy I will wear turquoise
And flirt with all the eligible men at the Moose Lodge
And I will be bright and fun
and smile at everything they say.
I will sing Karaoke and drink Chevis and water
And dance with whoever asks.
And after I have done all these things
I will get on my bright purple streamlined trike
and pedal home.

Susan Groves Peyton

SECRETS AND LIES

I love him ... my secret
He loves her ... his secret
She doesn't love anybody
That's no secret ... she just lies.
Secrets and lies
Broken hearts
Wasted lives
I can survive anything except
secrets and lies.

Stan Sujka
Winter Park

FOUNTAIN IN TIME

Elizabeth, the daughter of the Florida sun,
    her memory strolls Park Avenue,
    her hand in mine.
From her grade school, along Central Park, the tracks,
    to the fountain that calls her name.
Where Fourth of July concerts, picnics, art festivals, and parades
    sent smiles to her face,
    we walk together.
I can hear her laughter in the wind
    as it weaves through the leaves of the giant oak trees.
The steel and wood tracts pulsate through the
    heart of the town's park;
    they bring me back and forth to The Avenue,
    but can't bring her back.
The peacock, her favorite bird, walks lonely in the woods.
    I hear it's loud lament,
    along the shores of Lake Virginia,
    it cries.
Dragging his colorful cloak,
    it drops his pixie dust feathers along it path
    a reminder of a child and her beauty lost so young.
It's crown, bowed in sadness,
    the peacock, frozen in bronze, rests on its pedestal.
    Its water cloak whispers a prayer, hums a chant, or
    or maybe sings a lullaby.
Roses at the statue's feet,
    bow their heads in the mist of heaven's tears.
A rainbow, sprays color over the brick avenue,
    from the heart of the earth where she rests,
    kissing the heavens where her spirit soars.
A happy little girl, her memory strolls The Avenue,
    as the peacock fountain stands guard,
    over the place she loved.

Published in The Winter Park/Maitland Observer, August 7, 2014

Stan Sujka

RAIN

It seems to happen every day, summertime around 5 PM.
White clouds, like stretch limousines, creep along the sky.
They drape the sun, and grayness envelops the earth like a
black and white movie.

The air sizzles, you can taste the static.
Explosions like distant fireworks beat on my eardrums.
Flashes of light burst in the sky and I start counting,
"One Mississippi, two-Mississippi," it's getting closer.

And it starts.
The air becomes thick.
 Mist slithering in the air.
A light drizzle followed by spitting shower.

In the split-second, slashing rain
              pitting and pounding the ground.
The trees sing with delight as they dance with the wind
              trying to shake the droplets from their leaves.
The lush summer grass stands taller.

Puddles form to the joy of barefoot kids.
Flowers like humble servants bow their heads in thanks.

Then the sun shoots gold across the sky.
 It drills through the grayness and the clouds.
Speckled sunlight.

Then a prism of a rainbow stretches against the horizon,
A double rainbow if I am lucky.
I take a breath of the cool air
Ahh, just another Florida summer afternoon.

Tahron Watkins
Orlando Area

A SUNNY DAY

If every day was a "Sunny day,"
then what would a Sunny day be?

The answer ... It would be like everyday. I say this to
say, despite all your past ways, we have all had obstacles
in our pathways, and I choose to believe that life isn't just black
and white ... there are many shades of gray.

In the past you've been through it all, stumbles and pitfalls.
Even going on journeys blind through fields where the grass
is too tall, u still seem to make it through it all.

And that shows character. No, I'm not talking SpongeBob
or Patrick. They say big things come in small packages and in
you, with qualities so fine it's obvious that it all depend on how
u package it.

Pressure busts pipes, but it can also make a diamond,
in order for it to do that you have to put time in.

Time and patients ... If broken hearts were a medical condition
the emergency room would be full of patients.

Lord knows you have seen your fair share of scares,
and the craziest part is it hurt you the most because you care.

When I stare, right into your deep ocean after all the crashed
waves and commotion, I see your devotion.
Your willingness to face the weather head on, like a beanie.

You overcome the storms; you control the rain with your pain,
Your smile tames the wild. Your love melts the snow,
and you light up the world with your glow.

See, you are a Sunny day, and it's your bad weather
that allows me to appreciate your powers,
the nourishment from your sunshine to my flowers.

159

"Genuine poetry can communicate before it is understood."

~ T. S. Eliot

Joseph Perrone
Ponce Inlet

ORANGE RHYMES

It seems to me so very strange
That there are words Rhyme cannot change,
And which if tried could us derange.
Pray tell; no word rhymes with 'orange'.

But like a dog that's full of mange,
A sight that eyes find oh so strange,
So are words we can't rearrange
Or change, so they'd rhyme with 'orange'.

Does this concern them on the grange?
Are they not happy on the range?
No doubt, it does not them derange
To find no word rhymes with 'orange'.

This thought just makes me want to cringe
Or to go on a drinking binge;
My nerves are dangling on the fringe
Seeking words to rhyme with 'oringe'.

Oh my! I just now felt a tinge.
I knew they'd want my tongue to singe
And thereby stop this rhyming binge
To find rhyming words for 'oringe'?

There now! I've felt another twinge!
Will it my sanity unhinge?
Please help me stop this rhyming binge
I know! No word rhymes with 'oringe'.

Joseph Perrone

MY TYKE'S BIKE

Like a boat being pushed away from the shore,
To drift away, and to be seen nevermore;
A boat that, once its line had been untethered,
Would be gone with the tide fore'er unfettered.

So did I push my young daughter on her bike,
Wishing she was still small enough for her trike;
A bike whose training wheels remained on the floor,
Where I left them, knowing she'll need them no more.

Once free from my hand, she soon mastered the ride,
Swooping around, 'fore coming back to my side.
"See, Daddy," she said, "I can do it myself,"
While I felt obsolete and placed on a shelf.

It seemed just yesterday she was a small tyke;
Now, she's all grown, riding a two-wheeler bike.

"Twinkle" Marie Manning
New Smyrna Beach

WHEN ESTHER CAME CRUMBLING DOWN

Word spread quickly.
Esther had taken a beating.

We knew Charley was an angry tyrant.
Overnight his name notorious
As he sucker punched everyone in his path.

Yet who could have predicted that Esther was his target?
Even when we knew he was heading her way?

Some, yes some, saw the turn and fled.
Most did not have enough warning
To hide from the fury of his unstoppable rampage.

But Esther she was strong.
No one, not a single one of us thought that
She, who was ever present to meet our needs
Would need protection, too.

After his storm subsided
It was only then we all knew.
Collective horror, united sadness
When Esther came crumbling down.

Poet's Note: Esther Wall was much beloved by locals of New Smyrna Beach. Adorned with beautiful Graffiti; a known meeting place for surfers. Hurricane Charley and the others of 2004 destroyed her.

"Twinkle" Marie Manning

LOOKING LIFE IN THE EYE

The mirror in the hallway reflected the depth of her pain.
She stopped.
Looked closer at the stranger.
Questions ran rampant through her mind.

Who is this woman in the mirror?
Why the stain of tears on her cheeks?
What in her life, past or present, was wounding her heart?
How could she alter the image to one of joy?

She took a breath.
Then another.
Thinking.
Always thinking.

She acknowledged she was looking life in the eye.
The life that had led her to this moment.
It was her journey.
She chose every step.

Even when confronted with the unthinkable,
Where every turn was fraught with despair
And each consequence was only a lesser evil
She alone determined the direction forward.

As she would now determine the direction.
For her road to hold joy, she has to choose joy.
Was she strong enough to release the comfortable
Cloak of sorrow?
Would she finally recognize herself if she did?

Ryan Tilley
Altamonte Springs

A PARROT'S SPEECH

This is the moment words begin to fail:
When love evaporates with heat of day
As pressures life imposes seem like jail.

We all do search for perfect words to say.
The mind should never overrule the heart.
When love evaporates with heat of day,

Their self-deception makes them grow apart:
A dream deferred absurd as parrot's speech.
The mind should never overrule the heart.

They stretch for love, perhaps an overreach.
Their failures amplified by friends' success.
A dream deferred absurd as parrot's speech,

Their bird repeats a line with no finesse.
A verbal mirror mocks the two as one.
Their failures amplified by friends' success.

Their final sentence seems to overrun,
This is the moment words begin to fail.
Remember how the cotton candy spun
As pressures life imposes seem like jail.

Ryan Tilley

NOT THE LAST FULL MEASURE

Civilian hit was Jennie Wade.
The bullet pierced her heart.
Projectile, called a mini-ball,
Was tranquilizer dart.
She was in kitchen making bread.
She kneaded stubborn dough.
Her parents lost a child in war.
They witnessed afterglow.
Her body went to sleep that day.
Her soul as free as bird.
She left the town of Gettysburg
That morning, July third.
Who fired the shot that killed the girl?
Which side's pathetic aim
Did kill a lady, not a man
By piercing house's frame?
The smoking weapon's acrid scent
Repeated stench of Hell.
The North and South devoured bread
As manna, even stale.
Metallic taste of blood to drink
For birds, for ghouls, for men.
The Eve of Independence Day:
Their treason, final sin.
The soldiers dodged the cannon balls
And spat out blood or phlegm.
The rebels heard a song's refrain,
Republic's battle hymn.
A flag in soldier's calloused hands
Bemoaned the lack of breeze.
The birds had flown away from war.
They missed the buzz of bees.

"To read a poem is to hear it with our eyes;
to hear it is to see it with our ears."

~ Octavio Paz

Irina Lives
Orlando

CHANGING CHANNELS

I defined family by what I saw on TV,
Idyllic moments spent sleeping over at friend's houses.
My childhood,
Strayed farther away from an after-school special.
Estranged farther from my father,
Arranged so I'd not bother my mother,
Interchanged to be raised by my grandmother,
Deranged far more than I ever let you know.
The more you know,
I wanted those sweet moments.
I lived for the aftertaste a saccharine family would leave
on my tongue.
I wanted to be impossibly happy.
I wanted to change channels.
I wanted to be a Keaton and a Huxtable.
My Family Ties were tenuous,
My Cosbys were just for show.
Our Silver Spoons have tarnished.
Diff'rent Strokes can't polish what's been done.
The cast is gone, but here I am with Growing Pains,
And I'm still changing channels.

Shari Yudenfreund-Sujka
Greater Orlando

GROWING UP, FOR PARENTS

I could not go with them when they went upstairs.
I could not help them for fear that I would cry.
Everything in its place for almost twenty years to be taken
away.
Everything slowly accumulated over the years to be packed
up and moved somewhere else.
Artwork, book shelves, a bed, night stand, dresser, and a
desk were all there making up a well lived in room.
Artwork, book shelves, a bed, night stand, dresser, and a
desk now all gone.
Children moving out within months of each other.
Children growing up and away.
Children no more.

Shari Yudenfreund-Sujka

GONE

I remember.
At least I think I remembered.
Remember what?
Hmmmm....

I forgot that.
How could I have forgotten that?
I remember it now. Really?
Hmmmm....

Will they remember me?
I can't remember them.
Today I can remember them though.
For today. Maybe just for today then.

Cards opened and then forgotten.
Birthdays barely recalled.
My own age an enigma to me.
Anniversaries forgotten.

A screaming daughter for not remembering her dreams.
What about my dreams? Strange, did I ever have any?
Yes, I remember. Not wanting to be forgotten.
Remember me.

Another rough week of things to do forgotten despite the lists.
Forgetting to feed the birds and water the plants.
Sad, irritable, angry, scared, despair setting in.
Trying not to give in to it all.

Feeling like a cartoon character that at any moment there
could be a flash of light,
And poof, I am gone.
Remembered.
Forgotten.

Sarah Garvis
Groveland

OPUS

"Don't only practice your art
But force your way into its secrets,
For it and knowledge can
Raise men to the Divine."
                              –Beethoven

So it begins with touch of pen,
twirl of paint, this, that dream that is of now
forever stained to paper's ears and eyes,
united, one, no war here–silence, peace,

and hope in art; see it through,
see through it, force your way, as it has forced
to teach us–with a whisper, sound,
stroke of key and keys
a whole vibrating round

beyond the noise, a joy, a joy
to bring forth best of all that's slipped away,
the thinking, thought and truth prevail,
pressing on against the breathless hard,
to breathe of what could be

and not what has become.

Sarah Garvis

THE ARGUMENT
 for Gertrude Stein

Outlet, where art thou, outlet?

Nay far nor near
Maybe if one would think
Let's say not, then where
Nay, far out
How out, one mind may ask
Where inspiration may hit
Ay, may seem true but it is really
A certain place or time
Really it's determined
One mind may think
Don't be so choosy
Choosy? Now seriously
If I may–you think
It's place and time
But really it's a state of mind

Lanaka Gibney
Winter Park

FINDING MY SELF

Sprigs of spearmint,
lemon rinds melting upon liquid,
sugar-crystal-spun-torrent.
Refreshing, sweet Southern living.

Cascading light painting the door-way,
pizza place, frost-touched cup,
confetti streaming substance of sight.

Foot hits the table, alone,
and all else fades.
Well let's draw these curtains,
parasol's hint of blue,
cold shadows,
I'm not warm.

Stuffing my feelings inside me, it's no help.
I walk up to the door.
I haven't been anywhere, but now, here.
Shifting handle and incoming flood.

Selfless actions-Love.
Breaking tearing-Misery.
Vibrant soaring-Happiness.
Stolen day-Betrayed.
Cared for-Content.
Pricking conviction-Rage.
Brought a grin-Joyous.
Swept smile-Sadness.
Risen Rainbow-Hope.

So much more ... white light blinds.

I can't be numb as I'm warm.
Heart beating in my freedom.
I'm breathing. I'm alive.

Lanaka Gibney

BAM KICK-IN' IT

With a saunter and a trot I walk off.
Once thought I had to stay put.
Not with this door off the hinges-
flowing drum movement.
Bam Kick-in' It.
Left the heated scene, fear and shudders.
Hummed and laughed, hands grasped frosted substance.
Beset by the stressed, I chewed ice in my walk, my hair
wavered in the wind.
I've been straight chill-in' with a kick in my step.

They all see me but fail to flow.
Let down their stress and close the sunset.
Streams of light though there's darkness.
Had the final rays by my side.
They failed to flow, they ran away.

Night hasn't had me and I've stayed happy.
Some drum and bass,
but my own steps lit the way.

Straight chill-in'.
Perfect escape.

Stayed moving,
Bam kick-in' it.

Theresa Pavell
Port Orange

THE BACK DOOR

No one walks the path to my door.

Bright yellow dandelions are growing there.

I haven't the heart to pull them

Mother Nature seems to want them to grow.

Please, ring my doorbell!

I am home; I am here.

ICI!

Theresa Pavell

TRANQUILITY

A feeling of calmness comes over me.

I feel as though I have been here forever.

I feel the strength that the ocean brings

As it tosses the waves onto the sandy beach.

Am I frightened that someday

I may be no more?

Anderson Dovilas
Port-au-Prince, Haiti

WHERE I AM FROM

It's not a simple fact
When silence is booming behind mountains
You can't name it
If your senses got locked on the news

You can't name it
If you've never been in love
With an unexplainable feeling

Where I am from
The sun is a deep song
Sleeping on trees
Protecting hopes that flourish in tears

Where I am from
Dreams are cheap
Dreamers are hard to find
And the night is wide enough
To keep a secret

Where I am from
Love is a blind faith
Leading people to their destinies

I was born over there
Between religion and politic
Two concepts
That is killing the happy life
That people are sharing everyday

My country is not
Scientifically built
We forgive more than we can heal
Provide more than what's needed

Where I am from
Promise is treasured.

Anderson Dovilas

MY SOULMATE

To the window sharing sounds and hiding images,
My patience is a combination of faith and hope
That I ride when things look blurry.

I whistle a morning of self-love
Against dreadful feelings,
Wild emotions,
And sightless passion;
My life is a rose sweating honey among scary vibes.
My silence is a slice of peace,
My inner rhythms possess me.
I am faithful to my soul
I can't be the one you are looking down on.

I know how the moon dressed
When virgin went to sleep naked
If streets were bodies
My hustle would be one of its tattoos

Instrumental misery
Cold beats
Cloudy Joy;
To the river that glides on the rocks
Don't wait for the rain to nurture your flow.
Keep sliding
Keep grooving
There is a fresh skin in this poem
With curly words
Erotic verse
Nobody ever asks God
Why death is afraid of Art.

Alice Norman
Holly Hill

IN PURSUIT OF

We thought we had a handle on it
In the sixties
We had a symbol for it
We marched for it
We had a sign for it
We imagined it for the world
We embodies it
It was a part of us that was pristine
We spread it like peanut butter & jelly
We still pray for it
long for it
Americans today are dying for it
May we never cease
To pursue it
peace

Alice Norman

WHITE-OUT

throughout the cold windless night
numberless filigree flakes
blanketing the barren slope
donning red cross-country skies
the morn heaves hills of diamonds
framed by an azure sky
crouching breathless at the crest
enthralled in pristine peace
I push off into whiteness
tethered by my faith

Mary Jane Barenbaum
New Smyrna Beach

MY NOSE

I can smell a gas leak from a pilot light before I get in the house.
Open the windows! Turn on the fans! Get the matches!

The smell of impending rain blowing from hundreds of miles
west can't get by my nose. I think it's the smell of wet leaves
already being dried by the afternoon sun.

Onions being fried, grilled, baked or broiled tweak my nostrils
from the house across the pond. I can't stand onions!

I think you have the idea. My nose is perfect but one
dimensional. The other talents just tease the openings of my
pretty hood ornament and I pay through the nose. (No pun
intended, or maybe yes.)

I didn't smell out the wise guy car salesman. He sold me a
'58 Ford that never started again after I parked it in front of my
house for the first time.

How about the apartment manager that swore that the heat in
the register would start working the next day. HA!

I can't forget my trusted co-worker that sold me a bill of goods
and a chance on a pyramid scheme that I just could not lose
money on. Where oh where is my $500.00 dollars? (In his
pocket, no doubt.) A rather tense association continued for the
next twenty years with that sneak!

Then the worst nose failure of all. Picking my first two husbands.
The old nostrils took an extended vacation, that's for sure.

Now, in the afternoon of my relationship with this appendage, I
feel it finally got things right in the husband department. Maybe
some electrical impulse between the cerebellum and the sinus
shook hands and said let's work together on this one. I have to
say, my nose could write a book.

Mary Jane Barenbaum

AFFAIRS OF THE HEART

It was your yellow sweater.

You leaned back against the wall

one foot balanced your stance.

I walked then ran across the atrium

my high heels kept time, click, click, click

I tripped as I reached for you

buried my face in you

The sweater embraced me, swallowed me

We danced at the club,

A little drunk

Dirty, down low, hips rolling

His breath smelled of whisky

His sweat smelled of lust

I smelled of want

A hotel room

Kept the lights off

Went home, slept 'til noon

I think his name was James

Brian Vargecko
New Smyrna Beach

SONNET OF REPOSE

I dig up a lyrical girl from Cedarland,
Who says: You must move on, must endure,
Alight your
worry ... defy them, be grand.
Her female-lightening eyes now abashed, God pure,
Spurs memories of times when we danced;
Children's hearts whispering where passion's bred;
Where a fetching gaze was all, we were entranced.
Life won't begin again until we both lie a'bed,
Though I'll obey and toil to warily pass the years.
But to climb in and cover myself with this dirt!
As only everlasting life puts an end to tears,
And sweeter is the succor the greater the hurt.
I embrace my love once more and we share a final kiss
I cover her back over, and return her to bliss.

Brian Vargecko

TOO LATE TO SAY

She freezes lemon bars from funerals and why would you not?
A riotous accomplishment of cowardice
Killing yourself
Dante got it wrong filling his lowest rung
Rained out from fireworks
A citrusy chance in yesterday's Goldilocks Zone
Storm sucking Jupiter, big orange blossom
Saves the pigtailed girl
Her swallow of
Juice, sour she declares, screwing up
Her eyes scrunching her nose
Forever deciding its flavor
If I don't make a sale this week I get let go
Tell me Tennessee
In your Menagerie
Did you miss appointments on purpose
To write Laura so well?
I wanted to write a play today
And fool my wife I was working
God hears our prayers but we choose our path
Jesus' was on water
The flowers I eat are orange
When I'm short on porridge
And no food in the fridge or to forage
You can even get in the sea, they let you
The willets don't mind the sanderlings
And gulls don't give a shit
Abiding one rule only
Outta my way I'm taking it
I stay a long time; make a good meal
Of chicken on the grill, side of saute'ed veg
The trick is to have all three
Masculinity
Intelligence
Tenderness
When no relaying the story can convey

Rachael Marie Collins
Orlando

THE ORACLE DOWN FROM DELPHI

Materializing into 4 AM
She shuffles and staggers into the hum and smoke and after
hours
Mumbling what passes for curses or enchantment these days
Stone-faced she sways on the cobbles and offers to read my
palm
For a cigarette or the price of whatever it is that is propelling
her upwards.
Broken English bubbling over broken teeth.
I divine from the tarot of her face that whatever she has to say
I've heard before or drew from common sense and the bright
Prognostications of insistent, well-meaning friends
Nothing to do with whatever this girl is spinning into drained
glasses
Or into the fiery fog.

I tell her I won't have my palm read
I have faith in my skepticism, even now
In this ungodly hour.
Undaunted her apple bright mouth rounds out
Her voice mud thick and soil dark with promises
That he can make nothing of me nor I of him
If I dare trust the value of her wisdom or her
Cheap plastic beads that jangle like temple bells,
Promising me the fruit of love that will taste like clay
Clay that will mold desires that will bake in the heat of the sun
And trembling turn to ash
Leaving me hungry for flesh from orchards growing
In far flung towns by humble folk that would
Rather let you starve then feast on a New England lover.
My sleep will be murdered on operatic levels.
"I know" I say and sacrifice 200 crowns for the cab ride home.

Rachael Marie Collins

LAST RITES

Spring came late that year.
Hardly making an effort
As if all that blossom and bird song has become a real drag
A real sodding bore.
And the winter
Held on so tight it began to feel good
And would not let go.
Nothing ever came full fruit.
Snow grudgingly gave way to rain
Rain that fell in unapologetic buckets.
Torrential and terrifying lilacs into a coma.
The fair, Muccha faced maid stepped down, languid as an
afternoon
Not even having the decency
To look embarrassed
As she saunters in like its two rounds till the last call
Trailing the last tattered furs of winter
Silk shoes dangling from a crooked finger
Unblinking and cloaked from throat to toe
Barely raising the temperature.

Gary Broughman
New Smyrna Beach

GIBRALTAR

It's not easy being the other one,
The one who's buzzed through
The locked steel doors,
Into the moans and cries.
The one who's supposed to be Gibraltar.
Who is Gibraltar on the outside
But like the big rock itself
Is laced with fissures inside.

Yes, it's harder being the one
Locked behind doors of steel.
But everyone knows that.
Words of concern come daily:
"My heart goes out to her."
"Is she getting any better?"
"Tell me when it's all right to visit."

Rarely, just rarely, someone thinks
To ask, "And how are you?"

Of course Gibraltar is always solid,
Like a rock, on the outside.
Don't show the fissures, don't even
Begin to admit them. You know there are
More empty beds, waiting
Behind those locked steel doors.

Everyone asks about the kids.
They're worried. Counseling needed?
The kids say no, "Not if you're OK, Dad.
If you're OK, we're OK."

Of course Dad is OK.
He's a rock. He's Gibraltar.
On the outside.

Gary Broughman

MEDITATION ON THE SEASONS

Winter, spring, summer, fall.
The words roll through
My mind, over and again,
Silencing the moment
Like the seasons rolling up
The years quiet the din
Of life's daily chatter.

Winter, spring, summer, fall.
A parade in memory, pictures behind
closed eyes of changing trees
And a changing me.

Winter, spring, summer, fall.
The slideshow repeats over and again.
Bare limbs capped in white, and winter
coats capped by furry hoods, soon
Overtaken by pale green unfolding
on every branch, and me below running
free, renewed like the trees, dripping energy,
ready and able in a light spring jacket.

Now summer takes its turn.
My tree is draped in lush deep green
and the sun gilds bare young limbs
hanging free from short cotton sleeves.
And then too soon the leaves are orange
and red and falling day by day above a boy
In a hooded sweatshirt.

Winter, spring, summer, fall.
Breathe in, breathe out. Yes.
Still, and almost smiling.
Happy to remember.
Happy to be.

Dave Bennett
Winter Garden

LIVE LOVE XVIII

There's a bright, toasty,
crackling fire blazing
in the large stone fireplace
of this cabin
in the mountains.

I'm curled up on the couch
mesmerized by the dancing
golden flames.

My mind's eye sees you
snuggled up here in my arms.

Quietly we sit,
holding hands.
We turn and stare
into one another's eyes
for what seems like hours.

No words need be spoken.
We kiss...lightly...briefly.

Again our eyes seduce
one another.

Smiles form at the corners
of our mouths.

Simultaneously, a tear glazes
our eyes, forms single droplets
and flows slowly
down our cheeks.

They mix and become one
as we kiss again...
passionately!

We are warmed more by the energy
of our love than by the heat of the flames.

Dave Bennett

LIVE LOVE XIV

You don't send me flowers any more.
You sang that to me...
as we passed one another
along the trail.

You were with your new love.

You were carrying a bouquet
of wild flowers.

At first I thought
it was just
a coincidence,
even though it hurt.

I would still be sending
you flowers
if
we were still together!

Now, days later,
I'm haunted by the image
of you...passing me...
the warm rays of the sun
shining on your face...
the bouquet of wild flowers
in your hands...
your voice singing quietly
those words.

Would I be hoping too much
to think you were trying
to send me a message?

You love me, you love me not.
You love me, you love me not.
You love me!

Barbara Fifield
Port Orange

CHANGING OUR WORLD

Kids on skateboards at the park
Teens fly kites at the beach
Balloons float at a party
Oh, the freedom of youth!
No more am I carefree
We miss what we can't bring back
The spontaneity of youth
A world where wars can come and go
But we are insulated
Adults can worry
But children act on whim,
Innocent of the future
Yet I cannot go back to yesterday,
Only fantasize what can happen,
As adults we hold powers to change our world
But sometimes we do not alter it for the better.

Barbara Fifield

THOUGHTS ON WATCHING THE DON QUIOXTE BALLET

Dancers stepping to a pasa doble brings back
reminiscences of you Enid
watching this same ballet with me ten years, ago.

"I've never seen a ballet, before!" you say.
How expressive your eighty-six-year old eyes.
As the gypsies banged tambourines I remembered my
daughter, Mona, learning the fandango in Seville, Spain,
twenty years, ago.
Now, you've passed away to higher realms
Do you also watch the pasa doble there in a higher plane?

And, you, Mona, have long graduated to a career
out-of-state administering to sick and needy.
Perhaps, you slide CDs into your stereo and dance the
fandango on your days off.

But I can still enjoy gazing at the ballet in this theater
in Daytona and daydream about dancing the fandango
someday, myself.

Joey Solomon Everest
Winter Springs

ON MAMA'S PORCH

The air is pure under the indolent swishing of her fancy fan
unfouled by his hot sour dragon breath spewing bile.

On Mama's porch in the shade of weathered ceiling boards
cradled with low concrete walls there are no knives no fists.

She seeks nothing from this humble world
where losses are spoken in lines carved across cheeks.

I sway in a hammock not speaking my own damaged memories.
Mama chews mint from her rocky garden to aid her
troublesome tummy. Her mouth moves with *uh hunhh* or *praise
God* affirmations to secret thoughts.

Sudden breezes shove tall palms slapping for a moment like his
rash rough words.
Her sweet clear voice sings of an old rugged cross on a hill far
away and she waits for the day of her crowns.

Neither kind nor calm I need this hope from her
to borrow it until it becomes mine.
I simmer like her pot of stewed beef on the two burner stove.
Mint leaves will not help my burning gut.

She has no daughter just me by marriage. I'll do just fine she
says, sighing because her son is not doing just fine doing time.

We thought we knew him think we miss him
but relief is the truth that remains.

On Mama's porch we rest, safe for now in a cement womb.

Joey Solomon Everest

LOSING EVERYTHING

You didn't really plan on losing your hair
           not cancer
just cancerous stress
eating away in tiny mouthfuls
easier to swallow.

That morning
clumps of hair fell like red fur
covering the shower floor.

I'd never seen you as naked
as that day I opened the bathroom door
and saw you
staring
looking for answers
on the shower floor.

You never planned to lose a lung
           not cancer
maybe raising seven kids
always broke never knowing
If he would drink the money away or
save some small bit
in his easy-come easy-go kind of
           cancer.

I never planned to lose you
not cancer
just hopelessness
swirling down the drain
life falling out
on the shower floor.

Rosemary Volz
Ponce Inlet

FROSTING

When the moon still had its way with me,
       when I hulled strawberries and frosted cakes,
       you would not have left.
Not while my root cellar was filled and we could still
       make each other swell.
Why would you leave Our Lady of the Kitchen Sink
       who could feed the hungry, clothe the naked
       and turn water into lemonade?

Women grow old waiting
       for coffee to perk,
       bread to rise,
       ships to come in.
Women have been known to freeze
       while anticipating a thaw.

Remembering a purple summer in Oregon
       when you taught the boys to cast.
Those perfect hands
       testing the waters,
       throwing lines,
       tying lures,
as I watched through a misty window
       and prayed the trout
       would fight the hook.

Rosemary Volz

PLAY

Let's make believe the circus tent isn't empty
And the Flying Wallendas are performing without a net.
Let's pretend the bare-back rider is
Wearing her blue sequin dress and her red
Painted toes are gripping the back of a
Belgian horse that is covered with glitter.
Let's say she winks at us as she goes around.

Let's make believe we're on a picnic and
Your father is waiting to throw the ball around.
Let's pretend my mother is urging me
To have another piece of chocolate cake
But we decide to hold each other tight
And roll down the hill with our eyes closed.

Let's make believe the drought has ended
And the creek is bubbling over pebbles as
Old as eternity and as new as tomorrow.
Let's pretend frogs are croaking and birds
Are celebrating the Year of the Worm
And you put down your book and smile at me.

Let's make believe she didn't go out that night
That she had to wash her hair or clean out her closet.
Let's say you never laid eyes on each other
That of all faces you still chose my face
That of all arms you still chose my arms
That of all journeys you still chose our journey
Let's pretend I am your beloved and you are mine.
Come on let's play.
It's getting dark.

Elaine Person
Orlando

WITH WORDS UNSPOKEN ... *after Rilke*

With words unspoken
I rowed the open sea.
I landed on an island
made for you and me.
And with you I grew orchids,
roses, and magnolias.
Our senses satisfied,
then I went to hold you.
With words unspoken
my loving heart touched yours.
The rowboat was our bedroom,
our poster bed, the oars.
I let my fingers tell you—
there was no holding back
my love to gratify you
and keep your heart from lack.
With words unspoken
just like the open sea
I'll flood you with my passion
with waves that come from me.
I'll kiss your eyes when sleeping
your lips when you're awake.
Yet sadly, this is fantasy
All I thought of—fake.
With words unspoken
I watched you sail away.
Our love affair was broken
because I couldn't say
the words I felt inside me,
the sentences, the phrases.
You never knew my love for you.
My silent throat erases
the streaming, current feeling
that only I will know.
And so you loved another
and I let you go.

Elaine Person

WEATHERING HEIGHTS

Can you come with me to the heather?
Will you be my own true love?
Will you take me to wherever
the clouds will rise above?

We'll laugh and sing on the hillside
We'll roll down meadow's grass
We'll hold onto each other
and be together at last.

I'll make the tributary
a pathway to your heart
The rivers flowing by us—
a great new way to start.

As long as earth and mountains
As far as eyes can see
our love is like a fountain
that welcomes you and me.

As steep as every hillside
As deep as every sea
our passion grows inside of us
to last eternally.

So meet me on the heather
Kiss me in the glen
Love me and forever
we'll be together then.

Thomas Lee Rhymes
Oviedo

LUST IS AN OPTION

When dealing with renegade lovers
Lust has an amazing way
of calming one's Spirit and
growing one closer to
the Universe's heart.

It is a song of Joy
sung by tempestuous tenors
the music of the World
held in tender arms amid
the tears of innocence released.

Beyond mere Love,
Lust brings life to those of age
whose days are slipping silently by.
Where, but in the arms of a lover,
does Mankind exist and exist again?

Gently give way to Lust
it pleases only those who partake.
But - if it is not enough

there is always Love to
fall back upon.

Thomas Lee Rhymes

ON THE THRESHOLD OF ETERNITY
inspired by the painting of Vincent van Gogh, 1890

the fire burns cold against my body
the embers POP! and SNAP! — much like
my limbs and back each morning

the aching of Age has settled in my Soul
the days are as thick as the mud on my shoes

Where did I fail?
When did my hope, become my helplessness?
At what point in Time, did I miss the turning?
Was I ever given a choice? A chance?

the dirt from my hands becomes a stream of mud
clinging to my sleeves - as it mixes with my tears

eternity is drawing ever closer
and I am so tired, so weary,
perhaps, I shall not be able to
cross the threshold and enter

perhaps, I am already there

*"If my poetry aims to achieve anything,
it's to deliver people from the limited ways
in which they see and feel."*

~ Jim Morrison

Other Poetry Books Published by CHB Media

Poetry to Feed the Spirit
Poets of Central Florida, Volume One

Love and Other Passions
Poets of Central Florida, Volume Two

Seasons of My Life, Mary Jane Barenbaum

Activistic, Nena Larieze

Strawberry Albatross, Irvin D. Milowe

A Mighty Warrior is the Ant, Natalie Warrick

Two Car Garage, Peter Gordon

Eyes Open, Listening, Janet Watson

The Wide World Through a Poet's Eye, Phyllis Lober

Blue Mist, Donatella Cardillo Young

Looking at Life Through a Small Eye, Natalie Warrick

Along the Way, Joan Bonnell Clark

Florida State Poets Association Anthology Thirty-Two
Edited for the FSPA by
Patricia Stevenson, Elaine Person, Gary Broughman

> *"To have great poets,*
> *there must be great audiences."*
> ~ *Walt Whitman*

On behalf of our editorial team: Russ Golata,
Elaine Person, and Gary Broughman,
thank you to all the poets who
submitted their heart crafted work to
Volume Three of Poets of Central Florida.

To those who comprise the "great audiences"
which poetry requires . . .

Read and Enjoy!

CPSIA information can be obtained at www.ICGtesting.com
Printed in the USA
LVOW07s0805050615

441304LV00001B/40/P